January ... 2

For Rupert
with lov
Sara

SARAH ANN [illegible]

MODERN DAY SHAMAN®

Find a deeper connection with life.

Sharing channelled shamanic journeys, poems, affirmations and meditations to activate your higher self and your success mindset

For permissions contact:
sarah@sarahnegus.com

Cover design by Nataša Ivančević

Paperback ISBN: 978-1-7356711-3-0

Published by:
Serapis Bey Publishing
Literary Agent and Editor, Wendy Yorke
WRITE. EDIT. PUBLISH
www.wendyyorke.com

The names of the characters in this book have been changed for identity protection purposes and any resemblance to people, living or dead, is purely coincidental.

All uncredited quotations are the author's own.

All the shamanic journeys, poems, affirmations and meditations provided are channelled through the author.

This is not the truth.

It is my truth.

Take what touches your heart and leave the rest.

This book is dedicated to you.

May you find your way.

Contents

About the Author

Sarah Ann Negus is a modern-day shaman. She grew up in South London and has spent her life finding out who she really is. Her journey of discovery, in this her first book, takes you from lost to found in the most alternative of ways. Sarah's experience was not easy, but she believes that coming home to your true self does not have to be a fight or a struggle.

As a child she learned that not everyone saw what she did, and she hid her gifts. Coming back to them as an adult, she slowly remembered her purpose and promised to share them.

Sarah runs a successful mentoring and public speaking business working with entrepreneurs and executives who understand their energy is a powerful driving force for growth, both personally and professionally. She facilitates an altered state of consciousness for her clients which allows them to observe themselves and the world differently as a result. They take actions from a new belief system, which empowers them to achieve what they previously believed was impossible. Her clients typically say; "This has been life-changing".

Never be afraid of the dark.
Without it there is no light.

Praise for This Book from Other People

"Sarah Negus is the true definition of a master healer in this antidote for the crisis of modern life. Her memoir reads like a shamanic Elizabeth Gilbert. It is deeply moving, inspiring and leaves you with the practical tools to live your own authentic self. Insights on how to activate your potential come with tears, laughter and profound love, much like the experience of being in the room with the Shaman herself."

Agnes Kowalski, Wealth Therapist and Forbes Contributor

"I have had goose bumps all over me from the moment I started to read this book. Sarah takes you on a deeply personal transformative journey. She invites you to use shamanic energy to heal your life and activate the level of potential within, which you never knew you had. Her writing takes us deep. I would say deeper than any other book I have read before. And it is worth it. Each chapter brings a new level of awareness and healing. Sarah's voice is relatable and very powerful. I enjoyed reading about her own journey of massive transformation and her loving guidance for using the power of energy to transform anything we want. Accompanying meditations are worth their weight in gold itself. This book is a must-read for all spiritually-based people who sense there is more … a lot more."

Lenka Lutonska, The Extraordinary Growth Coach, Business Strategist and Mindset Maven

This book takes you into Sarah's journey of self-discovery so you can find your own. It is the path less travelled which is in itself fascinating. The reading of it allowed me to move past everything I knew and find something even more potent for my life in the most alternative of ways. This is a must-read for anyone looking for something more in their lives without knowing what that is.

John Paul Beeby, Celebrity Fitness and Wellness Coach

How to Use this Book for Maximum Benefit

When I first sat down to write this book, I allowed myself to be taken by the words. They flowed easily and the main body of the work found its way onto paper in 6 short weeks, helped by my writing coach Karen Roy, but it was not finished. Although it felt complete to me, the parts of my story that were relevant did not stand alone effectively. I had to dig deep to discover – with the help of my author coach and literary agent, Wendy Yorke – the teaching within my written words. I am eternally grateful for the help of both Karen and Wendy in bringing it all to fruition.

If you are reading this, it is likely you have aspects of yourself that continue to bring challenge to your life. My recommendation for you is ... when you identify them ... love them. Love really is the answer to everything. I use the word love here, not in the romantic sense based on condition, but love that builds and creates. Use this book to help you recognise these aspects within yourself more deeply so you can acknowledge and accept them. Then – this is the important bit – integrate them into your life as part of you. Aspects of yourself that are ready to be seen and transformed into something more beautiful.

In this book, I share real events from my life, unembellished. I start each chapter with My Story and its relevance for our modern world because my intention is to provide you with true stories that will resonate with you and evoke a remembering to bring a new recognition of yourself. In each chapter, I also give you a practical exercise to help you integrate what you learn about yourself. You will also find a client story illustrating the practical learnings other people have experienced. In several chapters, I provide channelled material as it was given to me, unedited and in places I supplement my story with my own channelled poetry. Finally, I provide you with a summary of the applications you can make in your life to give you a step-by-step path to follow on your own journey to activate your higher self and your success mindset.

As you dive into the content of the book, you will find a chakra cleansing meditation and eight unique shamanic journeys, which I have channelled. They hold an energetic charge to help you connect to their power and see more of yourself than you have seen before. You can repeat them as many times as you like because each time, you will find new information, which will help you explore your best self. I encourage you to read these pages with a journal alongside to record your thoughts, any memories that come to the surface, and to ground your journeying experience. I have my early journals and I continue to find new insights in them every time I read them.

This book's main message is one of: self-recognition; self-awareness; self-knowledge; self-compassion; and self-love. By knowing your 'self', by coming into yourself, and by acknowledging yourself as more than merely a physical being, you can find a deep connection to the planet, to your families, communities, and all the peoples of other countries. In fact, all the sentient beings who live here on planet Earth and to the whole consciousness of our Universe because we are all one.

My intention is that you find your place of safety, support, and love within and you contribute to the oneness that is longing for more love.

"When we are no longer able to change a situation, we are challenged to change ourselves."

Viktor Frankl, author *Man's Search for Meaning*

Prologue: Realisation

August 27th

How did I get here?
Who the fuck am I?
Is it okay to swear?
Who the fuck am I?
I guess it is okay to swear.
I feel better when I do.
It somehow gives emphasis to the fucking mess I'm in … there I did it again.
Everything hurts. My back, my neck, my arms, my right leg, hell, even my eyes hurt.
And my brain.
My brain cannot function.
It is having a meltdown.
I can literally feel it dissolving into mush under the immense pressure I feel looking at my reflection.
I am 30.
In fact, today is my birthday.
A happy day, right?
One to celebrate life.
One to bask in the spotlight of specialness.
A day to be spoiled.

A day to mark a significant milestone.
I have made it to 30 years of age!
I live in a beautiful home.
Have a gorgeous baby son, a husband who adores me, friends, family, material wealth.
Then why the fuck do I feel in so much pain? … oops, there I go, swearing again!
Blaming the car crash on my migraines and depression gives me some sort of excuse, but somehow deep in my bones, the bones that ache so much, I know it is not the reason.

I examine my face in the mirror. Close up. Smokey green eyes with long dark lashes framing them. Eyes that should be sparkly and alive but instead they are flat and stare accusingly at me. Midnight dark hair falling in tumbles to my shoulders. My grandmother's mouth. Full and red, ready to speak truth and wonder and smile, set sternly in a line. Regally high cheekbones, petite ears and a sweetheart chin. I knew I was beautiful, but inside I hid something else. Inside there was a deeply black crawling mess of ugliness that churned away. It constantly talked to me. Reminding me every day, every minute, every spare moment. I was fake, I was a fraud, I was stupid. I got what I deserved, nobody liked me let alone loved me. I was ugly, I was ridiculous, I was shameful, I was nothing.

I was not worthy of anything at all.

It was that inner me that looked out from my smoky green eyes, facing me squarely in the mirror, and spoke to me, boldly. *"I absolutely loathe you! I control you! What are you going to do about that?"* I do not have an answer. I shy away from looking at myself and turn to look around at the home I am standing in, unresolved, undecided, unloved. Instead, I sigh deeply.

Is this it? I thought to myself. *Is it my lot to continue living in this struggle to free myself from all this pain? Is life really this hard, this bad?* More questions I did not have the answer to. But, on that day there was a decision made. I looked up, talking to the ceiling, the heavens, a place far away in the Universe, talking to something I thought was bigger than me.

"Show me the way back to me."

This is that story.

Chapter 1

Time to Remember

"Human beings are not born once and for all on the day their mothers give birth to them, but … life obliges them over and over again to give birth to themselves."

Gabriel García Márquez

There are no coincidences. Everything is a nudge, a push, a jolt, a bump, or a crash to steer you on your path whatever that is, wherever it takes you.

My story: become the student

I am very stubborn. Sometimes, I do not listen even now. While in my early adulthood, I was completely deaf to the whispers of my higher-self – my spiritual essence –which seemed to be talking to me in a language alien and unintelligible. Then came Eve.

It was mid-summer. A hot, sunny July day. The kind you only find in south east England. Green and bright and humid.

The sunlight shining through the leaves of the trees dappling the grass. Birds singing at the top of their voices in the garden and bees buzzing in the lavender outside my kitchen. The phone rang, one of those plugged in, landline phones. My girlfriend was on the other end.

"Sarah, gorgeous, I'm going to see a spiritual healer. She's bloody expensive, so I wondered if you want to share the hour's session?"

"Of course, I would, Wow, of course I would."

"Great darling. I will pick you up in 10!" was her dramatic reply, with which she slammed down the phone.

This was in the days when my son was in kindergarten. I only had a few hours in the day without him. I did not need to pick him up until 3.30pm; I had time to go with her.

Excited, I clambered into her 4x4 and off we drove, echoes of Thelma and Louise on adventure came to mind. I was curious and had questions swirling around unanswered in my head. *What will she say? What will she know? What will I find out?*

We drove for an hour, singing out loud to the songs on the radio, enjoying the drive and the beautiful day. Taking a few wrong turns, but eventually arriving at a huge house, set deep in the countryside. A tarmac driveway with a few potholes led us to the car park and main entrance. A gothic-looking porchway opened onto a reception hall. It was understated in its décor; wooden flooring, an unlit fireplace and sunny yellow curtains dressed the hallway together with two comfy looking blue sofas. It felt imposing and cold despite the warm sunny day outside and I shivered a little as I entered.

Eve greeted us. She was a larger-than-life character with dark hair and even darker sparkling eyes; in her late 50s, full of certainty and confidence. She looked me up and down.

"Take a seat young lady, I'll deal with you later." Then, she bustled off with my friend in tow.

Apprehension started to overwhelm me, and my thoughts ran wild in my head.

"See, you are nothing. You are not important. Even Eve wants you to wait. Wants you to go last and she does not even know you. You will never be first at anything. You have to wait because you are not worth a thing."

The loud voice within me was playing up as I sat waiting my turn. It was noisy and persistent and liked to remind me often that I was not good enough to be noticed, that most of my choices were wrong and that I was silly or stupid or both. It was not clear to me where that voice had originated, it was simply there, filling me with doubt at every turn.

"I will forget it. I'll go and wait in the car. I do not like this place, it's cold. She is really scary. I do not like her. I'll pay her for my session, but I will not go in."

I stood up, ready to make a quick exit, right out of the door, out of the waiting room and back into the sunshine and the safety of the car. To go back to my predictable, flat, inauthentic life where my loud inner voice was in charge.

Change is sometimes more frightening than remaining in the comfort of the pain you know and manage on a day-to-day basis. This pain is habit forming, as is the managing of it. I was looking right down the barrel of the gun that would bring immense change. Somehow, I knew I was on the cusp of something big and my fear was palpable.

"Do not fucking do it," screamed the voice in my head.. As I got up to leave, as if by magic and exactly on cue – remember there are no coincidences and everything happens for a reason – Eve bustled out of her room, waved goodbye to my girlfriend, looked me up and down once more and said, "Right young lady. I will deal with you now. Come along."

Gulp. "*Do not call me young lady,"* I thought. *You are going to deal with me. How rude!* But instead of running away, I followed her to her office, my heart beating in my chest so hard I felt it banging against my ribs. My pulse was racing, perspiration breaking out on my forehead. *Could I be having a panic attack? What is this?* My chest was tight, I could not breathe.

"Fucking hell Sarah, what are you doing?" That voice inside me again.

My resistance was huge, but I also felt inexorably drawn to this lady. There was something about her I could not explain. I had never met her before. Until today, I had never even heard of her, yet somehow, someway, I knew I was in the right place. Exactly the place where I would discover new information and find truth.

She scanned me, nodding. Then suddenly, her voice changed and she dropped into what I now know was a trance and she channelled her message for me.

> "You are very unhappy.
>
> The child in you is lost.
>
> She cries often and you ignore her.
>
> Your body has become a cage, an armour to hide your heart, which is so wounded it may close completely.
>
> Your life force is weak and walks behind you for it does not feel this place is safe.
>
> You are gifted.
>
> You are hidden.
>
> You are light, but so dark.
>
> You are young, but old beyond your years.
>
> There is knowledge for you to learn well, but it is your wisdom that will change your world. The world.
>
> Time is the healer here.
>
> Experience your initiation and find your way.
>
> First, embrace your wounded child, find your vision of your life, for only when you are whole can you teach.
>
> I see you.
>
> I honour you.
>
> Shaman *Aho.*"

When she had finished, I realised that tears were streaming down my face. Tears of sadness.

Tears of relief. Tears of vulnerability. Tears of love and tears of recognition all mixed together.

This strange lady, this stranger –Eve – who later became my teacher, my facilitator, my memory provoker, had in the space of a few minutes told me more about myself than I had ever dared to admit. She had accessed my energy and channellled such strange truths back to me in a manner that was unworldly.

I continued to cry for two more days. I could not stop. Deep sobs wrenched from my body, held down for so long, breaking free at last. I felt deep depression, cracked open and raw. The people around me did not know what to do and I knew they could not help me. Only she could, Eve. With her sparkling eyes and promise of bone deep honesty. So, I went back to that weird cold house deep in the countryside. I went back to the lady who knew so much about me with so little to see of me and asked her to help me. She did and now I am here sharing my journey with you.

Meeting Eve was the first time I had come into contact with a real-life shaman, or as I had labelled her a 'crazy lady'. I had a confused idea that a shaman was the medicine man or woman only in the ancient Native American culture. I had another notion that a shaman was dangerous and messed about with evil spirits. Going back and asking for her help, even if she did look 'normal', was a leap of faith. This was one of the times in my life when I jumped off the cliff of habit and conditioning. I ignored what I thought I should do, leapt into the unknown, full of trepidation and fear only to find that instead of falling to my end, I was actually flying; soaring high into the sky with a new wider perspective of who I was and what I could become.

As it turned out, Eve was neither Native American, nor evil or dangerous. I say that carefully, because she did have a temper and you never quite knew when she was going to share it with you; she is human after all. Despite this, Eve possessed the energy of motherhood. The non-judgemental, unconditional love kind of motherhood and it oozed from every part of her being. She was a straight talker. If she saw something within you, she called it out. She could smell fake and sly a mile off and did not suffer fools, ever.

Eve was magic and I loved her. She saw what you were afraid of and she helped you to uncover it, so you faced it – all the while encouraging you to decide that tomorrow was always a new day and every new day offered the opportunity for you to be more you than you were now. There was no *status quo* with Eve. Only truth, laughter – she had a wicked sense of humour – ancient knowledge and wisdom. I knew she had taken the path less travelled and I was certain this was now my journey too.

Shamanism and its place in our modern world

I soon discovered that shamans existed in all ancient cultures far and wide around the world. In fact, my surname the word 'Negus' means shaman or king in the language of Ancient Egypt and continues to be used today in Ethiopia. The shamans of Ancient Egypt were their leaders. The Pharaoh held the spiritual, physical, and emotional health of their people and were initiated into the wisdom of the traditions passed down through generations. (A good description for the role of the shaman in every culture.)

Shamans were found all across Asia and the world. The word shaman was first translated into English in the 17th century when it was brought back by a Dutch travellller and statesman, and ambassador to the English court, Nicolaes Witsen, the first explorer to Siberia, the Far East and Central Asia. The word shaman was included in his 1672 book, *Noord en Oost Tataryen/North and South Tatary.* The word, as we know it, is said to have originated from the Tungus tribe of Northeast Asia. In English it means spiritual healer, one who sees in the dark or one who knows; a 'doctor of the soul'.

The shaman traditionally was a visionary, prophet, healer, psychotherapist, ceremonialist and often an herbal doctor. He or she cared for the health of their community by looking after the spiritual and physical health of its inhabitants.

For me, the word shaman means many things.

- Open
- Curious
- Searcher
- Adventurer
- Pioneer
- Seer

But the word that resonates most for me is 'bridge'.

Shamans are bridges between the spiritual and the physical. They are able to travel through many realms to see into what appears to be darkness to find the light. I am forever grateful to the shamans I have worked with who saw the light in me and helped me to shine it more and more brightly.

Shamans see themselves in other people. They can expand their consciousness past what is proven and known and can telepathically communicate across vast distances, to people, animals and even to our planet Earth.

Shamans:

- translate spiritual wisdom;
- gather spiritual energies;
- are conduits of divine love;
- bring shades of grey in between the black and white of situations; and
- uncover different perspectives, different beliefs, and different physical experiences for their clients and the world.

This understanding of the label shaman has come to me only after many years of experience. When I first began exploring this ancient art, I was curious and accepted what I was shown on a surface level. I did not question my insight when I was journeying. The experience was real to me. More real than my physical existence and it was much more fun.

I wanted to find out how to translate that 'fun' into my real life. I began to decipher the energy of shaman. I wanted to explain to other people my passion for energy and my calling to share this philosophy.

I remember when I first set my stall out on the Internet, having decided that hiding away in Surrey in the United Kingdom was 'playing small'. I began to join international groups online where I tentatively shared my spiritual gifts. Over the period of about six weeks, I facilitated 150 free hour-long sessions. Each session with a stranger. Each one on a conference call without the client physically present. Each one powerful.

I had been sceptical as to the shifts I could evoke in distance work with only my intention, my ability to travel in energy and my spiritual insight to guide me. The first day, I held 10 sessions and at the end of them, I was buzzing. Buzzing with energy, convinced I was on to something big. I knew without doubt that I was connecting with the spiritual energy of my client. Interpreting symbolism they saw in their mind's eye. Bringing them to a place where they changed their deep beliefs about themselves. What was more, I understood that when I travelled with my clients, I was accessing more of myself. Inspiring my clients – unconsciously – to go the extra mile, to stretch a little further, to risk more of themselves. They broke down and shared secrets. They uncovered old unhelpful thoughts locked within them and witnessed the beauty of their soul in ways they never had before.

At that time, I was calling myself a spiritual mentor. It was not until a number of my clients began to describe me as 'their shaman' that I took on the description. This is traditional. I had not been been given the honour by an indigenous tribe, but by my own community, those people who knew me and had experienced my energy and my work. They understood what I was. My Western tribe of clients named me shaman. I added 'Modern Day' because that felt aligned to working with modern people, facilitating change by accessing parts of their energy that they could not. A shaman is the bridge.

Channelled Poem: I Am the Bridge

"I am the bridge.
The way between now and what could be.
The arch of possibility.
The link between realities.
The place between conscious and unconscsious.
The rainbow that connects to your pot of gold.

If you are curious.
If you feel you are more than you seem.
If you say yes to yourself.
If you are brave enough to be good enough.

I am the bridge.
The pathfinder.
The way seeker.
The door between all you have been and all you can be.

I am the bridge
Come journey with me."

Shamanism is a philosophy, a way of being, a way of living, a search for knowledge of self and of the Universe through, and by experience.

Shamans can be found in Inuit, Amazon, Norse, Native American Indian, Mauri, Ancient Greek and Roman, Ancient Egyptian, African, Asian and Aboriginal cultures.

The Aboriginal name for their shaman is 'clever fella'. A fella who sees what other people do not, who knows how to translate the energy of the divine and connects it to the world.

A 'clever fella' does not look at a person to see what they have acquired in life. They do not look to see how their personality translates to what they buy, their clothes, car, home or career. A shaman looks into a person's eyes, the mirror of their soul, to see how deep their awareness of themselves goes. They look for distortions of energy and for emotional blocks that hide the person's light. They understand how to sidestep the cultural conditioning that is part of our world's physical reality. They look straight into the web of energy that connects us all and brings hope, acceptance and answers to problems so solutions can be found. They bring an invitation to become what and who you really are.

During the last 22 years, I have played with the idea of shaman. I am non-traditional, which means I did not become initiated in an indigenous culture before the age of 30. I do not have roots or physical ancestry that leads back to an indigenous elder, but I know I am shaman, The Modern Day Shaman®.

The way of a modern-day shaman is to bring reason for the chaos of Western life. In coining this description of shaman,

I come with the knowing that spiritual information is to be shared. It is for all of us, so we can find a better way, if we choose.

A modern-day shaman does not walk into the wilderness to find themselves as the ancient and indigenous people did and continue to do. They do not need to, for the life we live here in the West casts us into a jungle of its own.

I understand that jungle first-hand. It is the jungle that swallows you and highlights that you do not matter; that you have no value; that you must work your fingers to the bone to succeed; and that success is measured by how much money you have. That jungle is bogus. It is materialistic and it kills the spirit.

During my childhood, teenage years, and early adulthood, I knew I was different, strange even. I thought this difference was a bad thing. I thought I needed to change, to fit in, to be normal, in order to be accepted. I thought I had to bury all the things I knew to be liked. I thought I had to please everyone around me and put my own needs, wants, and beliefs to one side so I could make other people happy.

I learned early on to hide what I saw beyond our reality. I learned the 'knowing' I had was not tolerated in a little girl. It was not acceptable. I learned to hide my light.

The deep belief I held within me was heavy to carry; . I was wrong, phony, an imposter, not good enough for love, not good enough for success, not good enough for anything. Only other people could be what they wanted because they were liked and loved. They joined in among society easily. I did not and I decided I was delinquent.

That, coupled with all manner of difficult experiences in my life, further embedded this belief.

The thing is, stealth or hidden shamans, shamans who are not yet on their path, not yet aligned to their truth, experience life through a distorted lens, with disrupted energy and an inability to settle or find peace.

There are certain signs to watch for, signs that mean you are ready to explore shamanic energy for yourself.

- You have always felt different with a knowing that you do not belong in the everyday and yearn to find other people who resonate with you.
- You can often feel lonely among a crowd of people. You enjoy your own company most.
- You can experience sensory overload and need time alone.
- You have been told you are too sensitive. This sensitivity is, however, your gift when harnessed effectively.
- You may sleep a lot finding that when you are well rested life is easier.
- Addiction to external forces can be a problem. You try to numb yourself with food, alcohol, or drugs as a way to get through the day to day.
- You enter into unhealthy relationships to prove to yourself that you are worthy, to prove you can be accepted. This can happen again and again on

repeat.

- You are often ungrounded. This is because shamans are able to expand their consciousness beyond what we have been taught about space and time in our reality. Finding a way to cope with this disconnection leads back to numbing yourself.
- Being in nature brings you back to yourself. It feels like home. Shamans are the link between the planet and the rest of humanity. Shamans anchor spiritual light and understand the Earth is our mother.
- You may have experienced many life lessons and find you are good in a crisis. These are our Western world's shamanic initiations. They have taught you compassion and empathy for another person's plight.
- You know you can be more than you are. You feel a calling for purpose and want to make a difference in the world.
- You give to other people who need advice but find it difficult to set simple boundaries, meaning you over give and feel burned out often with resentment building within you.
- Dreaming is vivid and you receive information for yourself and other people.
- You know things without having been taught them. This is the slow remembering of spiritual truth that happens as you awaken to your path.

- You have 'magic hands' and find your touch soothes other people tremendously.
- People tell you their problems, off-loading their troubles, unconsciously knowing you will have solutions for them.
- You often think of things happening and they manifest.
- You may suffer with physical problems. This is called Shamanic Sickness. Hidden shamans are prone to many auto-immune disorders such as chronic fatigue, ulcerative colitis, fibromyalgia, Lyme disease, chronic pain, depression and sudden traumas such as car crashes. Ahem… this was me, until I accepted my path.

When I began working with Eve, I did not know I was shaman. I had not embraced the idea. I was busy ignoring most of my spiritual self. I did not see myself as someone who would eventually leave their comfortable lifestyle to reinvent herself.

I thought Eve would help me heal myself. I had no notion that I did not need healing; after all I was a mess, actually a hot mess, but healing was not what I needed. None of us do. We need to be able to see our own truth and embrace our path and enjoy our journey. So often we are searching for a destination, a nirvana, that already exists within us. That beautiful heavenly place is in our own heart. It vibrates from our soul and is a part of our being.

The first new practice Eve taught me was shamanic journeying, drumming, and trance. I did not know why she was teaching this to me. I believed it was for me to feel happier, to be more content and to live my life as a better wife, daughter, mother, sister, and friend. How wrong I was! She was teaching me – with an intention – to pass on tradition, to invite me to remember who I really was and why I had lived my life so far.

One of the most powerful of my early journeys is forever etched on my memory. Shamanic journeying is a very real experience. You actually go 'there'. Your experiences stay in your memory in the same way as a great day out does.

On this day, I found myself in our shamanic journeying weekly group, with my eyes closed, my palms turned upwards in my lap, back up straight and my feet firmly planted on the floor. Within my mind's eye, I clearly saw myself stepping on many ascending columns of light, going higher and higher and further into the spiritual dimensions than I had ever been before. I was getting cold and the chill was distracting me a little. Gently and carefully, I felt someone place a blanket around my lap, the safety and warmth it gave me allowed me to continue.

I saw more columns of light all leading to a high ledge. A deep black ravine opened out in front of me defined by another ledge opposite me. I stood waiting. Wondering what the next verbal cue would be from Eve. This time there was none. I waited. Alert. Listening. My third eye opening wider and wider, until I saw him. A huge male energy dressed in blue with golden hair. His beauty took my breath away, as did the overwhelming feeling of love washing over every part of my form.

"I am Michael" he said.
"You have to jump."

I realised he meant jump across the ravine. Well, I was not going to do that was I? Eve had not told me to. I did not know Michael.

"Jump!"
He said again and then, "trust!"

Suddenly, I did. I could not stop myself. In my vision, I jumped as hard, as fast and as far as I could. I found I was on the opposite side of the ravine. All that I had needed to do was trust; set the intention; and it was done. Clearly, a lesson I needed to learn in my life.

Now that I had jumped, a knowing developed within me. I was in the presence of Archangel Michael, a powerful spiritual being whose name means, 'He who is God.' He leads the Archangels, the group of angelic beings who help humanity evolve towards love.

He took me by the hand and led me into the golden energy I saw all around. He showed me how far I had come along my path; invited me to honour all of my experiences so far. To not blame, or judge but to see the lessons learned. Then, he showed me the light that is connected to me and I was, and continue to be, humbled.

That journey was the first time I realised my abilities to hold energy, to travel through dimensions and to match energetic frequencies other people cannot. That journey was the first time I wanted to be able to do more, to help more, and it was the first time I knew I would be more.

I began to understand that my difference was my gift. That my gift was important, precious and something to nurture and grow.

Like a small child in a candy shop, I began to try all the different flavours available to me in the energetic realms. From vibrations that caused nausea and muscle tightness, to energy that flowed and moved like rivers, and frequencies that played out like beautiful music.

I heard the angelic choir, which translated into layman's terms is a group of angelic beings singing love vibrations, which touch your heart and soul, and give you a feeling of completeness.

I felt the belly-wrenching pull of gravity and grounding, which can feel so heavy and overwhelming when coming back from an energetic journey into the reality of our physical life.

I time hopped. To explore past lives and future selves. Finding myself in ancient places that held resonance for me and then transporting me to hopes for my future.

I played in my mind's eye with mythical creatures. Pegasus, the winged horse and mermaids who swam with me in the ocean.

I discovered how animals could come into my awareness both in my physical world and in the spiritual world to bring messages through. Black Panther is the spirit animal I associate with my sense of personal power. She walks by my side energetically and helps me find my courage. Once, I remember noticing hundreds of geese all grouping together in a farmer's field. An invitation to be brave and stay loyal to myself.

I got to know my personal spiritual guides. These are energetic vibrations that come close to us to help on our life's journey. It brought me great comfort to know I was never alone and supported in ways I did not understand or see.

I found emotional trauma, however seemingly insignificant or infinitely terrible, caused different distortions in the energy of a person, rather like a knot in a ball of string left untended and tangled. Unravelling such trauma, following it back to its beginning, recognising it, understanding it, and forgiving its existence weakened the power it held in life today. That, coupled with uncovering conditioned beliefs taken on from family, society, culture and experience, can unlock physical armouring. These are habitual postures adopted by the body as a protection from the drama of emotions. Once released, a new level of living can emerge and take shape. Not only in the physical body but in every aspect of a person's existence.

That is the language of a modern-day shaman. And, in shamanic tradition, I confirm my explanation with, *Aho,* which means 'to clear' and is used to affirm an intention or declaration.

Reflections

Personal growth is a life-long expedition. It never stops. Even when you feel stuck, or feel you are treading water, going around in circles, or going backwards in your life, you will be growing and changing day-by-day, breath-by-breath. It is inevitable. We are here to overcome what we think we should be, in order to become our true selves. The first step is to realise there is more of you and for you, than you are aware of now.

Noticing that you are stuck, have relationship patterns repeating in your life, or you feel miserable despite everything around you looking amazing, is when realisations hit home.

A realisation that you need to evoke change within you is powerful. Often, you will have tried to change many other aspects of your external life. You may have learnt new skills, or left a job, moved home or country, only to find after the initial adrenaline rush, you soon fall back into flatline, the same habits and the same way of feeling not quite your true self.

This is an invitation to look within. The common denominator here is you. External situations, people, events, and challenges force you to look at yourself and grow. You are the only aspect you can change, the only aspect you have power over and deciding to change yourself is the biggest gift you can give yourself.

Changing yourself means becoming aware of hidden beliefs and recognising habitual thoughts which are running in the background of your life. They are difficult to notice and can be addictive, often creating a plethora of unhelpful self-talk that feels normal.

Our lives are governed by a high proportion of unconscious patterns. Our behaviour, moods, energy levels, and general happiness and productivity, are ruled by what is happening inside us. Most of the time, our thoughts are automatic, automatically negative, automatically self-critical, and automatically too busy. As this is something that has always been so, it remains so. We do not question these thoughts. They carry on regardless, bungling along repeating the same patterns of behaviour every day, while we remain unaware that we could find more time to be happier each day.

One practical way to raise and expand your self-awareness is through a daily practice of Free Writing. This means that every morning, before beginning your day, you write down whatever words want to come out of you, without worrying about the sentences, or spelling, or format of the writing. Relax and write whatever unconscious thought patterns are ready to be transmuted from within you onto your paper. This action allows unconscious self-talk to become real. It does not take long but is a powerful daily emptying of the mind.

Every morning before you climb out of bed, reach for your notepad and your pen and allow your unconscious thoughts to pour out of you onto the paper. Write three pages in all, every morning without thinking. Allow words to tumble onto the page.

The very action of writing whatever comes spilling forth releases space in your mind. These writings are not for re-reading or analysing. They are a tool with which to clear clutter from your psyche. You will probably notice a theme to the scribblings, this theme is something you can become aware of and work to understand and change. The main thing is to let the writings babble, let them rumble, let them rip. They will probably surprise you.

If nothing comes easily, begin writing; 'I don't know what to write' over and over again. I promise by the end of the first set of three pages, you will have surprised yourself and unlocked many thought patterns.

If you have ever felt the benefit of de-cluttering a garage, or a kitchen cupboard, or a wardrobe, begin your day by de-cluttering your mind. Find space within that can be filled with more useful, positive, and in-the-moment feelings. See this outpour as an aspect of life that contributes to bringing a smile to your face, in contrast to the To Do List, which might have been the prominent thought.

Free Writing is a simple way to uncover what lies beneath your 'normal' and is the first step towards changing you.

David's story: from burn out to daily celebration

David came to me feeling burnt out. He was a high-level corporate executive running a team of 25 staff. He loved his job and reported feeling alive and vibrant when he was 'on top of his game'. However, that exhilarating feeling had left him and he was exhausted. When I asked him to describe his inner narrative, he looked at me blankly. 'I don't have any' was his answer. Something I questioned and invited him to explore.

He was ready to feel better and having tried therapy, gym work-outs, a promotion, multiple girlfriends and exotic holidays, he realised he was the common denominator and was open to finding an alternative way to improve his life. I invited him to Free Write for two weeks and to report back on his findings. He was resistant at first and it took two days before any information flowed onto the paper of his three daily pages However, when they did, it was a true revelation for him. Through his daily writing, he revealed how he was incredibly mean to himself, constantly comparing his successes with other people who he saw as 'better' than himself. He never allowed himself to rest, always pushing himself on, and always demanding more. He recognised he was never happy with his performance, his inner mantra being 'it's good, but not good enough'.

The start of his Free Writing activity was the tip of the iceberg. It gave David insight into his inner belief that he had to work hard, harder, and hardest. However, his true realisation came a month into this daily practice.

He suddenly recognised the energy of words he wrote on the pages of his free writing as that of his father. He was pushing himself to prove his worth to his father and to the small child that felt unseen, unheard and unloved unless he was top of the class, captain of the team and leader of the many. He understood that he was taught he could do anything he put his mind to, as long as he worked hard. The small child had taken on this truth and saw working hard as never stopping until you were exhausted, the young boy had watched his father work every day at a job he hated, the adolescent had yearned for his father's praise and to spend time with him only to be disappointed when his father chose to work (hard).

As a result, he decided to work hard on himself, to get to know what he really wanted to be in life. This was a big step for David. He had spent his life achieving in action and inner work is all about achieving peace of mind and spirit in being. He decided he had nothing to lose and had become so uncomfortable in his life that he was ready to make big changes.

These changes were life changing and far reaching. In the short term we spent time discovering David's core beliefs around what he had to offer. It became clear that he was living in the past, playing out habits of behaviour learned from his family. We had to find authentic David.

Our inner truth can be shocking. David's was. In the space of six months he changed everything in his business world. As we delved into his subconscious mind via shamanic journeying David connected to the spiritual sense of himself. He felt powerful in his own mind and body, he came to a knowing of success in being himself, his best self, not one designed by his parents or his culture or his corporate career.

David was very brave. Something his father had taught him to be. He courageously dismantled how he had been existing in life and began to experience shifts that allowed him to feel free.

Shamanic mentoring is a partnership; David and I built a relationship of trust, I showed him what he could not look at within himself. Together we unravelled the tangles of 'shoulds' that he lived by, and built new beliefs based on a vision of his future life, and his future self. I invited him to live with his future self in mind, offering him curiosity as his main driver. He loved that, took the bull by the horns and began to ask himself questions.

What do I want?
What do I need?
What can I see for myself?
What am I not?
What is unhelpful?
What are my strengths?
What are my weaknesses?

Who am I now?

Who do I want to be?

What legacy do I want to leave and to live?

These were big questions, and he embraced them by finding excitement in the journey, feeling the benefits in his health, relationships and everyday being. Over a period of two years he left corporate life and began his own business as a consultant. His work life balance improved as did his inner dialogue, allowing him to celebrate his wins in the now and to enjoy his work and the rewards it bought him.

Practical applications

- Recognise your repeating life patterns.
- Acknowledge your own feelings within them.
- Listen to your inner dialogue and bring it out into the open.
- Accept it is you who has the power to change.
- Decide to look within.
- Free Write every morning.

Chapter 2

The Rainbow Within

"We live in a rainbow of chaos."

Paul Cézanne

The first time I was presented with the notion that I had energy centres within me I settled into cynicism. This reaction was interesting, especially because my early childhood was filled with sights of magical creatures, which I could not explain. I had buried that part of me so deeply and had taken up the mantle of the sceptic so well that it was hard to shake off.

The Chakra System

I was in a room full of people at Eve's country retreat, 12 to be exact. All being asked to describe which colour of the rainbow they felt most drawn to. Eve had created large disc shapes on huge pieces of paper. Each one painted with a colour. Red, orange, yellow, green, turquoise, indigo blue, and purple. Apparently - *"Yeah right"* said my inner cynic - each colour represented a different energy centre within the body.

These energy centres dealt with different ages of development, different qualities and emotions, which can get wounded and blocked.

I rolled my eyes up towards the ceiling.

"Really."

"Come on."

And in the words of my dad, I said to myself, *"You have got to be kidding!"*

I wanted to believe. I knew when I put my hands onto areas of my friend's bodies that I felt different energies and so did they. I thought this was coincidence or the Placebo Effect; the effect of the mind believing something, so it happens. On this particular day, I was a 'nocebo'. My mind did not believe a thing.

I grudgingly admitted I liked the purple circle best. I felt a sense of peace when I looked at that colour. Some of the group liked green, some turquoise, it was purely individual preference.

Eve nodded wisely and looked through me as I spoke about this. She paused and said to me, "Rather than resisting this through judgement, open yourself up to this possibility. Perhaps there is something for you to learn here?"

As usual, with only one sentence, she managed to stop me in my tracks. She was right, I was resisting. Stuck in my stubbornness, wanting to stay in the right lane with the rest of the world, when she was inviting me to take a turn and go left.

Ultimately, I was afraid. Afraid of change. Afraid of finding myself in a completely different world, one where nothing was fixed or real. A world where everything was available. A place full of information that was not learned academically. This world, this universe was made up of energy, vibrating, sparkling, multi-coloured energy that flowed through me and was me. It collected along my spine in energy centres that vibrated and rotated. It ran through my whole body. If I was honest, when I was quiet, when I was in my stillness, I felt its hum.

These energy centres are chakras. The word chakra means wheel. Chakras give, receive, store and flow. Once I surrendered to their possibility, the idea of them captured me. This system of energy has been handed down through the ages. Originally, through the oral tradition of the ancient Indian Brahmins where the word wheel was a metaphor for the sun. An eternal wheel of time representing celestial order and balance. The idea set me into a romantic tailspin of wanting to know more.

Ancient people thought we had rainbow colours within us mirroring the stars and the sun!

"Oh my!" I remembered reading Dante Alighieri's "The Divine Comedy". The final verse touched my heart.

> "But by now my desire and will were turned,
> Like a balanced wheel rotated evenly,
> By the love that moves the sun and other stars."

"Oh my!
Could this energy be love?
Could it be love moving everything?
Could it be in me?
Love?"

I was beginning to understand that coincidence was never coincidence. These matched experiences were perfectly timed to show me I was in the right place, on the right track and to trust all the new information I was learning. Parallel to this, I was battling an ever-growing choir of disgruntled voices in my head.

I am from South London. Croydon to be exact. An area that was edgy, some might say it was a bit rough. We used the 'F' word a lot, for example.

While I was having these realisations with one voice in my head, another voice in my head, rather colourfully, was inviting me to, *"Fuck off and remember that no one loves you."* It was a loud voice. It was difficult to ignore. At the time I did not really have the tools with which to deal with it. I let it talk, swear, shout, jump up and down, stand on its head and distract me. Sometimes, I managed to ignore it, but often the voice took over.

My interest was piqued when it came to the chakras and I started to read about them. I gathered every book I could get my hands on. I discovered that the seven main chakras named within the body all corresponded with a major nerve plexus along the spine. These are areas of the body where groups of nerves branch out from the spine, spreading out to send messages to the arms, legs, and organs. I understood this was a physically powerful place; nerves move our bodies. The research I uncovered showed the chakras were placed energetically in corresponding areas of the body. I was fascinated.

In her book, *Anatomy of the Spirit,* Caroline Myss wrote,

"Every thought and experience you've ever had in your life gets filtered through these chakra databases. Each event is recorded in your cells".

This got me thinking even more.

If chakras were really like databases of information, surely you could access that information, add to that information and in doing so affect not only the energy of the person, but the physical body as well.

Then, I had what is coined as an 'Aha' moment.

All of my life's experiences were stored in the energy in my physical body. I was a walking, talking, feeling, experiencing, energetic library and research centre, all tied up in one body.

Me.

That 'Aha' moment was the first time I realised I was special. I had value that was not tied to money. My experience mattered. I finally got it. No one before, nor anyone after would contribute to the world like I could.

It was as though something had lit up within me. I felt an effervescent golden bubbling at the base of my spine expanding into my body and amplifying the hum of energy that was already there. It felt like champagne bubbling up once its cork had popped. I felt alive. I felt connected. I was not separate. I was supported. I was loved. Hell, I was love.

I felt the mini chakras in my feet reaching down and pulling me strongly into the Earth. I recognised the mini chakras in my hands opening, ready to receive information and to share the energy flowing through me. I sensed my red base chakra opening and linking me to the planet, my ancestors and all that I had learned from my family.

Without a strong, open, base chakra it can be difficult to ground any spiritual information. There has to be a root. A tethering to what came before and a connection to where we live on Mother Earth. The base chakra can be tightly closed in many people. Early childhood can feel alien to a newly born spiritual being. Opening and balancing the base is something that allows energy to flow. Prior to my 'Aha' moment, I had been too grounded, stuck, heavy, there was openness but no flow. My sacral chakra rocked and rolled a bit. It was a muddy orange instead of a beautiful terracotta. I knew there was wounding and blocking there, in particular. Something I would spend a long time dealing with as the years went by. The sacral chakra, located in the pelvic area, is the seat of our relationship with ourselves. It holds information from our first relationships. Those exchanges experienced through the eyes and hearts of an emotionally immature child. This chakra can hold a lot of baggage. It plays a big part in how you hold relationships with everything in your life, people, food, and money. Boy, did I know I had some work to do here! My relationships with everything were dysfunctional to say the least.

I found my solar plexus interesting. It was either wide open – so open that everything and everybody walked all over me in my quest to be liked and to fit in – or it was shut, tightly closed, with boundaries so rigid there was no movement at all. Remember, I said I was stubborn. I knew this was where I found courage, where my self-esteem was defined but I could not find the energy to help this yellow chakra shine.

Then I came to my heart chakra. Rigid. Closed. Low energy. So quiet there was no movement. This is the green energy centre and when it is healthy, when it is open, the green is so soft and beautiful that it completely beams love. It is the gateway for spiritual information to flow into the whole system. Allowing desire – with the help of the base chakra – to ground and manifest into something that feels real in our world. It seemed mine was dead. Where was my self-love? Where was my self-compassion? Where was my self-forgiveness? Non-existent, absent and hidden. It was a revelation that I had none of this self-love within for me. I found these qualities for other people but not for myself.

Then the throat chakra, which is traditionally gorgeous turquoise. I saw this energy centre as turquoise and gold but mine was black and cracked. I never dared to speak my truth. My heart was so broken it was difficult for me to find any sense of what speaking compassionately and with empathy was. I kept my mouth shut. I said nothing and then played out every conversation I wished I had spoken, silently inside my mind. Holding unspoken conversations within is toxic. Words hold vibration, as do thoughts. When they are not expressed, they distort the energy flow dramatically. It is better to speak, or at least, to write down what you wish to say. The throat chakra is also the centre of creativity. When there is maturity in self-expression, creativity can evolve.

The indigo blue of the third eye looks like the inky blueness of the night's sky. When I first looked into mine there was not much there. The darkness frightened me. The power of it gave me a feeling of tightness around my chest. The vastness of the unknown in this chakra left me feeling small and insignificant. This is where insight is gleaned. This is where wisdom and intuition entwine and dance and offer knowing that is not learned and sometimes not even understood.

This chakra is where I now explore the outer reaches of the Universe, this is where I sit. In my third eye, on a stone ledge, dangling my feet into the void. Gazing out in the velvet energy of the Universe. Picking out pathways and portals, shining lights of energy and many other things. Today, this chakra is my haven. Back then, it was my hell. I only ventured there with guidance, a hand to hold and a steady heart beating beside me. My insight had been the main thing that caused pain in my past – knowing too much without knowing why. This anomaly was a significant reason to disconnect and close off from this gift of mine. Even now, my third eye can blink closed momentarily. When that happens, I know I am on the brink of a big shift. I understand I will be guided, once more, to go left when everyone else thinks I should go right. Now though, I trust myself and I obediently skip, hop and jump off to the left and wait to see what is coming.

Red, orange, yellow, green, turquoise, blue. Oh yes, the crown chakra. Exquisite purple, turning to white. Opening like the petals of a flower into the consciousness of the Universe. Reaching out tendrils of energy, connecting, communicating and drawing in. As my third eye was closed tight, my crown was wide open. Unbalanced and ineffective. How could it work? My heart chakra was dead and my lower chakras were popping and combusting. I loved the feeling of expansion that I got in my crown when I could find it. Most of the time my higher mind and any spiritual connection got lost in mind chatter; the choir of unhelpful voices that I gave space to within me. Mind chatter is debilitating. It is common when the third eye is closed, yet the crown wide open. The ability to bring spiritual information down into the body is severely limited. That was me, then.

In those early days, the rainbow within me was 'off'. There was no balance, no framework for health. Some energy centres were blazing with colour, others dark and grey. As I learned to connect with them, I noticed certain chakras had an effect higher up or lower down in my system. Their health, I realised, affected how my physical body was feeling. Lower back pain and sciatica, something I was rehabilitating after a car crash, flared up when I spent time exploring my sacral chakra. Migraines came on full force when I pressured myself to speak my truth and share my spiritual insight. My habitual round-shouldered posture, which I did not enjoy, accentuated when I spent time sending love to my heart. My heart chakra was my most wounded, it took many years to coax it open.

Chakra health is an ongoing moveable feast. Your chakras respond to your beliefs, emotions, thoughts, actions, posture and intentions. They are rejuvenated in sleep and dream time helps them as you process your life unconsciously.

I often journey into the chakras with my clients. They are great places to explore. Sometimes they show up in the journey all dusty and dirty, neglected and needing cleaning.

Sometimes they turn up crammed full of objects, people and situations ready to be let go. Other times they can be a source of adventure and information. They are always a way through the veil separating what we are conscious of and what lays latent in our subconscious.

The chakra system always benefits from attention. I advocate spending focused time clearing and cleaning each chakra, daily. Here is a Chakra Clearing Meditation for you to practice; a symbolic exercise that works with your intention. If you would like to listen to the audio version of this journey you will find a link at the back of the book.

Chakra Clearing Meditation

> Close your eyes.
>
> Sit up straight with your hands relaxing in your lap.
>
> Palms turned upwards to receive all that you are able to at this time.
>
> Call your energy to you from wherever it is in the Universe, the world and your life.
>
> As it collects, settle it into your midline; that deep central part of you is the crystalline calcium bony structure of your spine and your skull. It is the electrical impulses of your brain and your central nervous system. It is the pathway of your chakras from your base, to your sacral chakra, to your solar plexus and

heart, your throat chakra, your third eye and your crown.

Get a sense of how you feel right now. Accept what comes implicitly without question.

Feel your feet connecting to the Earth and notice your crown chakra being present to the heavens.

Feel the space behind your eyes.

With your intention come down into your base chakra.

Right down at the bottom of your spine to your tail bone.

You can feel this chakra underneath you as you sit. It is red. It is a circular disc and rotates clockwise. Allow it to open up and spend focused time breathing into this energy. Your intention is health. In your mind's eye you see the energy being cleaned and cleared and becoming more vibrant.

Ask the question, How can I ground and connect more fully in my life?

Accept whatever you receive in answer.

Feel the space behind your eyes.

With your intention come down into your sacral chakra.

You will find this in your lower abdomen. You

can feel this chakra in your lower back. It is orange. It is a circular disc and rotates clockwise. Allow it to open up and spend focused time breathing into this energy. Your intention is health. In your mind's eye you see the energy being cleaned and cleared and becoming more vibrant.

Ask the question, How can I build a loving relationship with myself?

Accept whatever you receive in answer.

Feel the space behind your eyes.

With your intention come into your solar plexus.

You will find this at the bottom of your ribcage. You can feel this chakra where your diaphragm sits. It is yellow, a circular disc and rotates clockwise. Allow it to open up. Spend focused time breathing into this energy. Your intention is health. In your mind's eye you see the energy being cleaned and cleared and becoming more vibrant.

Ask the question, How can I have healthy boundaries in my life?

Accept whatever you receive in answer.

Feel the space behind your eyes.

With your intention come to your heart chakra.

To the middle of your chest. You can feel this

chakra in the beat of your heart. It is soft green, a circular disc that rotates clockwise. Allow it to open up and spend focused time breathing into this energy. Your intention is health. In your mind's eye you see the energy being cleaned and cleared and becoming more vibrant.

Ask the question, How can I love myself?

Accept whatever you receive in answer.

Feel the space behind your eyes.

With your intention come to your throat chakra.

This is in your neck. You will feel this chakra moving as you turn your head. It is turquoise, a circular disc and it rotates clockwise. Allow it to open up and spend focused time breathing into this energy. Your intention is health. In your mind's eye you see the energy being cleaned and cleared and becoming more vibrant.

Ask the question, How can I speak my truth?

Accept whatever you receive in answer.

Feel the space behind your eyes.

With your intention go to your third eye.

You will find it just about your eyes. You can feel this chakra in the middle of your forehead. It is indigo blue. It is a circular disc and it rotates clockwise. Allow it to open up and spend focused time breathing into this energy.

Your intention is health. In your mind's eye you see the energy being cleaned and cleared and becoming more vibrant.

Ask the question, How can I receive insight?

Accept whatever you receive in answer.

Feel the space behind your eyes.

With your intention come into your crown chakra. You will find this on top of your head. It is purple, opening up to white. It is a circular disc and it rotates clockwise. Allow it to open up and spend focused time breathing into this energy. Your intention is health. In your mind's eye you see the energy being cleaned and cleared and becoming more vibrant.

Ask the question, How can I connect to all that I am?

Accept whatever you receive in answer.

Feel the space behind your eyes.

Feel your feet connecting to the Earth.

Feel your body on the chair.

Notice your breath moving in and out of your chest.

Take three breaths. When you are ready, come back to this place and this time.

Aho.

As you will have felt in this meditation, your intention is a powerful thing. It creates change. Makes things happen. However, we do not use it effectively in our day-to-day life.

Here is one particular journey to illustrate the power of intention. It shows how you have the power to change your emotions and therefore, your energy. If you would like to listen to the audio of this journey you will find the link in the back pages of the book.

Shamanic Journey One: Understand the Power of Intention

> Ensure you are sitting comfortably. Either on the ground with your legs crossed or on a chair. Your palms are resting on your lap turned upwards.
>
> Feel the space behind your eyes. Notice the presence of you. Your consciousness.
>
> You look without physically seeing. You in your knowing.
>
> In your mind's eye come into your midline the place where your spine is. Think of its line from your tailbone up to your neck and skull.
>
> Link with the electrical impulses of your brain and central nervous system and then, settle into the pathway of your chakras.
>
> From your base that you sit on, up to your sacral chakra in your lower back, to your solar

plexus beneath your diaphragm, to your heart in the middle of your chest, and to your throat.

Then, to your third eye in your forehead and finally, to the crown at the top of your head.

Settle here.

Connect to the rhythm of your breath and feel how it moves your body.

Feel the space behind your eyes.

Follow the spiral of your spine down from the inky blue of your third eye to the turquoise of your throat. Through the green of your heart and open to the sunny yellow of your solar plexus. Allow this energy to open out and around you so you are surrounded by it.

Take a breath and exhale.

In your mind's eye, the scene changes and you find yourself in a cave. There is light shining down from above and you feel safe and supported here.

You see mirrors in front of you, full length mirrors standing side by side in a line.

They are beautiful, ancient and framed in gold.

You step in front of the first one and see your energetic body.

Your physical reflection falls away. Only your energy is mirrored back to you.

You notice the line of chakras in the centre of you and watch as they rotate and glow while you breathe and think.

You observe the lines of energy flowing from their pulsing movement into the rest of your energetic body.

You see strong flowing areas and closed tight areas.

This is you in a neutral observing state.

You step in front of the next mirror and set the intention to observe the emotion of anger.

This emotion flares up in your energetic reflection and you notice how it feels and its impact energetically.

Recognise how easily and quickly you chose to feel this emotion and how it affects your energetic chakras and the flow of energy to the rest of your body.

In your own time, you step in front of the next mirror and set the intention to observe the emotion of sadness.

This emotion affects your energetic reflection and you notice the feeling of it in your body and see what it does to your chakras.

Recognise how easily and quickly you chose to feel this emotion and how it affects your energetic chakras and the flow of energy to the rest of your body.

The next mirror is for the intention of happiness. When you are ready, step in front of it.

What does your energetic reflection look like in the state of happiness? Observe how easily you moved from anger to sadness, then to the state of happiness simply with your intention. Watch how your chakras open and close depending on the emotion you have chosen to feel.

The final mirror is for the intention of peace. You step in front of it. Your intention shifting your emotional state once more.

Spend focused time here. Inner peace is wonderful. Watch how your energetic-self responds to this quality.

Feel the space behind your eyes.

Settle into your physical body.

Connect with your breathing.

Notice its rhythm in your body.

Set the intention to allow inner peace to maintain within you.

Send this intention down from your crown to your base following your midline.

Go further with this feeling sending it down out of your base and out of your feet into the Earth.

Ground the intention and invite it to stay in your body and in your life.

Your chakras are the rainbow within, they are the gateway to your energy, not unlike the rainbow that leads to the pot of gold.

Take a breath in and exhale.

When you are ready come back to this place and this time.

Aho.

Paying attention to your beliefs, thoughts and emotions paves the way towards self-knowing. It is easy to wander through life half awake, but there will come a point of no return, when a choice will be offered. Stay and slowly fall into the unease and ultimately, the *dis*ease of disconnection to your soul's truth. Or, pick up the baton of exploration and go in search of your heart. If you decide on the latter choice begin with your chakras. Learn all you can about how they work within you. Understand that whatever you know now will change; be forever curious for more information. Becoming the master of your own life starts with diving into the inner world of your energy. Follow the rainbow within you; it may feel like chaos, but in chaos there is always creation.

Reflections

Your energy centres, chakras, store experience and move emotions through you. They are a vast library of information that you can utilise in your quest for self-knowledge. Becoming aware of their energetic flow and listening to what comes through to your inner knowing when you clear them will show you areas of your life that can be explored and improved.

Susan's story: from dysfunctional relationships to love

Susan came to me wanting to find love in her life. She had been married, was now divorced and had a number of difficult relationships since. She found it difficult to be honest about her needs and therefore never really showed up authentically, instead moulding herself to what she thought her lover wanted her to be. Her boundaries were non-existent, and she found herself going to events and socialising with people that did not feel comfortable or fun. She was always helpful and giving, so much so that she often felt resentful when all she did was not acknowledged or rewarded by those around her. She self-medicated with the odd glass of wine or two. She yearned for a significant other, someone who would match her, be her equal and her partner in life.

I could see her sacral chakra was tight, the energy of her life-force quiet; her solar plexus was wide open and loose, her heart chakra guarded, and her throat chakra clogged up with unspoken words. We worked together to find out what she really wanted to feel in a relationship. She listed all the qualities and attributes her partner would have: honesty, trust, love, laughter, strength, connection, intelligence, acceptance, support and safety. When we looked within, Susan realised she first needed to cultivate these qualities in herself.

She became aware that she did not trust her inner knowing, she was not honest about her needs, she looked for love externally and was actually mean to herself internally. She did things for others to be noticed. Her strength was aligned to holding on, and holding in all that she felt, and she did not accept herself or support herself or hold her spirit safe in her own heart.

Susan began a journey with me to change all of these things and in doing so began to behave differently with the people she met. She let go of old difficult friendships that perpetuated her old way of being and found that new people entered her life. Within six weeks of writing her relationship wish list she met someone who became her partner and three years later her husband.

Practical applications

- Spend time clearing the energy of your chakras.
- Listen to your inner voice as you do.
- Journal the information.
- Set your intention for the life you want.
- Take action by changing how you show up in your life.

Chapter 3

The Power of Animals

"If you talk to the animals, they will talk with you and you will know each other."

Chief Don George

Understanding spiritual symbolism

The gardens at Eve's healing centre consisted of acres of lawn and woodland opening out towards rolling hills and farmland. Beyond the formal lawn of the house there is a gathering of oak trees. They stand together touching boughs as if holding hands like children singing "Ring a Ring o' Roses". They create an informal circle within the reach of their canopy. Their trunks giving a boundary to the round. These trees though, are not childlike, they are wise. They have stood and watched the ages unfold as they stay steady rooted in the earth, reaching to the skies, giving shelter to birds, squirrels, insects, and beetles. They offer shade on a hot day. Something to lean against when thinking and companionship for anyone feeling lonely. They have a manner about them offering a sense of containment. In the middle of the round is a fire pit where I have spent many an hour watching a fire twist and twirl around charred wooden logs. Quietly talking with companions or simply enjoying the language of the flames. This place is special. If I looked around, with the eyes of the little girl within me, I am sure I would see tree spirits and faeries around the outer-edges where ancient daffodils grow and bloom spectacularly in spring.

On this day I was busy with a group of people. We were building a sweat lodge. I did not really know what I had let myself in for. This was my first 'sweat'. I thought it would be like a sauna, hot, with rocks and a bit of discomfort. I do not like saunas at all. I was here because Eve wanted me to experience one and because of Mark.

Mark was a pioneer of shamanism in the West. He brought the teachings to the United Kingdom in the 1980s, after exploring the philosophy in the States. He was an eccentric character. He had a shock of white hair, a full white beard, a hat and a quiet stillness about him, which I found disconcerting.

There was not much stillness in me. I was too busy questioning myself. The mind chatter track at this particular time was along the lines of, *"Are you nuts? You are going to sit in a tent with strangers, in the dark, wearing only a sarong to pray and chant. Do not tell anyone because they will cart you off as insane!"*

But, like a good girl, I desperately wanted to please my teachers. I helped to tie the willow withies together to form a low dome-shaped structure. Then, we threw tarpaulins and blankets over the roof. These came all the way down to the ground obscuring any light.

My inner voice was chattering on, *"I bet the Native American Indians do not use tarpaulins or blankets. I bet they use authentic skins. These coverings will smell and scratch. You better get out of here before you have to go through with this. Go on! Leave. Make some excuse. Tell them you are ill. Tell them you have a headache. Get out of here!"*

I did not. Mainly because I knew Eve would see right through me. She would sense the energy of my excuse and call me out on it. I would look like a fool. It was much better to shut up, put up, and endure this, so I did. The threat of Eve was bigger than my inner voice that day. I trusted her. She said this would be good for me. She said it would clear many things. She said it would open up my channel. All things I wanted. I had experienced a few intuitive hits; they were exciting and extraordinary, and I wanted more. This was why I was there. To find more, to be more.

After a few hours work, the sweat lodge was ready. The fire was built and was burning away, heating the rocks. The fire was set to the east of the lodge with a trail in the earth connecting it to an altar – also to the east – outside the lodge. The alter was a simple oak log with foraged flowers and pinecones together with tiny pieces of paper holding the written energy of our intentions. The trail in the earth continued into the lodge connecting to the fire pit within it.

In a sweat lodge, there is a Chief, the leader of the sweat within the lodge. There is also the Fireman, the person who stokes the fire and ensures the rocks used within the lodge for heat are ready. Eve was the Space-holder. She was the guardian of our energy. She would not take part but would be present with us all throughout the four parts of the sweat. These four parts are called doors. They link to the four elemental directions of east, south, west and north and offer respite to the intensity of the heat within the lodge. Each door marks the end of one part of the ceremony, a sign the next phase of the experience is ready.

We began, standing around the fire, calling to the elemental powers of the four directions and the powers of creation, Mother Earth and Father Sky, to support us in our quest.

Mark blessed the lodge with a burning sage stick and cedar oil. We lined up to be smudged. A burning bundle of sage was wafted all around our bodies, clearing our energies. I took off my clothes. We were naked apart from sarongs wrapped around us. I submitted to the smoke and then crawled into the lodge.

Once inside, it is tradition to make a prayer 'for all relations'. An acknowledgement of the greater good. The experience within the lodge, being not only for the individuals taking part but for all – the universal consciousness – the ancestors before and ahead.

During this prayer, I realised the sacred nature of the ancient ceremony. This was a privilege and I needed to take it seriously and be present.

Time passed. It was dark, pitch black dark. It was uncomfortable. We were sitting on the ground with only thin cotton sarongs around us. I had chosen mine thoughtfully. It had animals printed on it and it reminded me of nature. It was not doing much of a job of resisting the scratchy grass poking through, however. The lodge inside was getting hot. We passed the time singing, listening to Mark's drumming in the heat.

"Hot rocks!" was the shout that went up periodically when Mark thought we needed more heat. This also meant we would be joining each other in another round of intention sharing. Meaning each of us stated loudly what our intention was for this sweat.

It was my turn.

"To find me," I said.

"*Aho*" answered my companions, acknowledging and affirming my words.

I felt shy, small and insignificant here in the heat and the darkness. Unsure of what would happen, how to be and what to do. My usual behaviour of checking out what I thought other people expected was not going to hack it. No one cared. Everyone was focused on their own experience.

We came to the end of the first door. We were invited to go out if we needed to. I did not want to. I decided to stay and find out what this was all about. The second and third door continued to build the intensity of the heat in the lodge. We sang. Mark drummed. The sweat lodge is said to represent the womb of Pachamama - Mother Earth - and I could understand why. I was hot. I was uncomfortable, yet I felt held, cocooned, safe.

We came to the fourth door. The heat within the lodge was intense, sweat was pouring off my body. I lay down and Mark took us into a journey, he invited us to open our third eye. It felt easy here in the blackness of the lodge without any physical distraction. My body had long since ended its battle for me to give up and go outside. My fight or flight reflex had let go of its hold on my soul. Here in this place, with this collection of strangers, I surrendered. I let go of all that I had been trying so hard to be and let the light of me into my awareness.

I felt my third eye first. A kind of itching in the middle of my forehead. Then, I saw it opening, light flooded in. I was standing in the brightest light I had seen in my entire life. More than blinding, yet I was not blind. It had a texture, a fineness to it. It gave me the feeling of the most exquisite art. It had a sound like a piano tuned to perfection and a feeling of the softness of the most luxuriant silk. Words simply do not give justice to it.

I bathed in it. Gloried in it. Allowed it to wash over me, flow through me and as I did the light began to change. The face of a huge black panther came bursting through. Its eyes were blue, its mouth open, its roar raw and overwhelming. I blinked, trying to blink it away. It did not disappear, instead it roared louder.

"Fuck. What is that?" I thought.

The roaring turned into words.

"I am your power, your personal power, your self-esteem.
I walk beside you, yet you do not notice me.
I see into the shadows where other people fear to look, yet

you prefer not to know.
I know what is hidden, yet you stay hiding in plain sight.
I am the truth you have not claimed.
Find the courage to be the bridge".

Then came snake.
Green and solid, its tongue hissing.
"I am your life force that you neglect.
I connect you to your primal instincts and to Earth.
I bring healing and transformation if you choose to receive it.
Find me in your midline.
I rise from your base through to your crown.
Your fear distorts me.
Surrender and trust.
Honour this in you".

Then eagle.
White eagle, its wings spread wide, its beak strong, its eyes yellow.
"I am your higher self.
All that you know.
All that you are.
I soar high above and see all there is.
My vision is wide. Yours can be too. Look beyond what you think you know.
I lead you.
I guide you
You are me on Earth."

Bump!

I felt my body bounce on the Earth inside the sweat lodge. I opened my eyes and focused on the faint glimmer of the last hot rocks glowing in the centre of the fire pit. It was hot. I was burning with energy, filled with passion and life. I could see in the dark, with my eyes open.

I crawled out of the lodge and lay face down on the cold ground. Time had stood still inside the lodge but not outside. The sun had set and the moon and stars were out. I rolled over onto my back enjoying the cool damp air on my body. I looked up and saw the shape of the Great Bear constellation – also known as the Plough or Big Dipper – clearly above me. It was blinking in the heavens, winking at me with the most knowing of winks.

What were all these animals about? I had seen and heard Panther, Snake and Eagle while in the lodge and now I was looking at the Great Bear, clearly marked out above me in the sky.

After drinking a lot of water, eating a hearty meal and having slept soundly through the night – with my curiosity exploding from my heart – I found Eve and Mark and asked them to interpret for me, to give me some answers.

Power animals, they explained, are part of our guidance system. They are spiritual energies we interpret and translate based on our human framework of what we know. Every power animal has a message, a positive and a negative. They bring information and guidance. They come through when we are not listening to our inner being. They are a way to distract the ego, the conditioned self and they connect us with a sense of knowing often missed.

We can call on power animals to help us in specific situations. If you see more than three animals together take time to sit and see if they have a message for you.

Some power animals stay as our companions throughout our lives. The three which came to me while in trance within the sweat lodge continue with me on my path today.

You will see your spirit animals in many different ways, in meditation or journeying. In symbols or imagery, which is how Great Bear first connected with me, in the constellation that twinkled above me in the sky. You may read of one in a book you have picked up randomly or you may see groups of animals or birds in unusual circumstances.

Crow is a big part of my energy. Whenever I see crows in unusual groups, I know that magic is happening. Their gathering reminds me to trust the magic. To sit back and wait and see how things will unfold.

Elsa, (as I have named my black panther), gives me a real strength of purpose. She never allows me to hide, always guides me to the root of every problem and is one of the most beautiful sights I have seen. The roaring of her power in that first instance of recognition was exhilarating, terrifying, captivating and an experience that is burned into my consciousness. I am never alone with her walking beside me. Even the darkest nights of my soul are lit up by her. My personal power, my ability to see what other people cannot, my comfort in the shadows are qualities I came here to share. Without Elsa symbolically holding this energy I would have continued to be afraid.

Now, connect with your Power Animals using the guidance below. If you would like to listen to the audio you will find a link in the back of the book.

Shamanic Journey Two: Welcome Your Power Animals

Close your eyes.

Sit up straight, with your hands relaxing in your lap.

Palms turned upwards to receive all you are able to at this time.

Call your energy to you from wherever it is in the Universe, the world and your life.

As it collects, settle it into your midline. That deep central part of you, the crystalline calcium bony structure of your spine and your skull, the electrical impulses of your brain and your central nervous system.

Follow the pathway of your chakras from your base, to your sacral chakra, to your solar plexus and heart, to your throat chakra, your third eye and your crown.

Get a sense of how you feel right now.

Accept what comes implicitly without question.

With your intention reach upwards from your crown chakra to the highest places in the Universe and bring down into your energy unconditional love.

This vibration passes through and expands into every chakra from your crown to your base.

From your base chakra reach down to Mother Earth requesting connection, home, anchoring and feel her presence holding you.

Settle and breathe. Allow the breath to fill and empty in your chest.

Feel the space behind your eyes.

In your mind's eye and with your intention come to your solar plexus. The seat of your self-esteem. Allow this energy to open around you. Bathe in the sunny yellow energy of this chakra.

Notice a door within the yellow. It is wooden. It has a clear quartz handle. You walk towards it and push the door open, stepping through.

The scene changes.

You find yourself in a meadow. The sun is shining, the sky is blue. There are white clouds floating above you. You hear the musical sound of a stream out of sight.

A path opens up in front of you. It leads you through the meadow into a woodland. The trees have a high canopy and sunlight lights a pathway. You follow the path until you find yourself in a clearing.

In the middle of the clearing is a stone altar. You walk towards it as a column of light comes through the trees and pools over the altar. You sit on its centre and the light floods over you.

Enjoy this light.

With your intention ask to meet your spirit animal.

You wait. An animal approaches from the trees at the edge of the clearing.

You smile and bow, the animal comes to sit with you.

Whatever comes, acknowledge and accept it, for it will have great information for you.

Recognise this aspect of you and give thanks for it.

Spend a little longer here with the animal that has come through.

You may ask questions.

"What have you come to share with me?"

"How can you help me in my life today?"

"What problem can you help me solve?"

Here, in the clearing you receive the light of universal love, breathe into the magic of the place, notice how you feel.

The animal moves away and invites you to follow, guiding you through the woodland to the stream you heard earlier.

You see a boat waiting for you. You climb in.

You bid your animal farewell. It is always here, to be found in your solar plexus. You may return whenever you wish.

The boat moves off down the stream. You enjoy the bobbing of the boat, the sound of the stream and the warmth of the air around you.

The boat continues along the stream and passes under a bridge.

The scene changes and you find yourself back in the sunny yellow energy of your solar plexus within your physical body.

Feel the space behind your eyes.

Settle into your physical body.

Connect with your breathing, notice its rhythm in your body.

Set the intention to allow a feeling of deep connection and grounding to maintain within you. Send this intention down from your crown to your base following your midline.

Go further with this feeling sending it down out of your base and out of your feet into the Earth, rooting the intention and inviting it to stay in your body and carry through into your day.

There is a general understanding that each of us has a number of power animals all assisting us on our path.

Spend focused time in the energy of the journey and invite different power animals to enter your awareness.

Aho!

Reflections

We have all the answers we need within us; what is tricky is listening to our inner guidance. Often doubt will overcome inner knowing with 27 reasons why not. A power animal is specific to you as an individual and offers beautiful ways to side-step conditioned responses and fear. They speak symbolically, bring calm, and soften resistance. They are never the whole picture, nor the perfect answer, after all in our life of discovery it is more about the questions and the exploration than it is the resolutions. Animals are all around us in the World, sentient beings that occupy this planet with us. Their energy contributes to us hugely. Love them.

Ben's story: the cynic

Ben was a cynic. A man of few words, he was humouring his long-suffering wife by visiting me. He submitted to one session only. Are you getting the picture? Ben did not want any help from me at all.

I asked him why he had actually even attended the meeting.

"I hate to waste money" was his growled reply. He was a big man, over 6 feet tall and well rounded. In his late 50s, proudly bald with blue eyes. Blue eyes that stared at me, warning me off.

I am used to cynics. I do not try to persuade them that I have anything to offer. I simply show up confident in my gifts. On this occasion my next question got Ben's attention.

"What is Bear for?" I asked.

Ben looked startled. He swallowed and shuffled his feet.

"There is Bear in your energy". (When talking of power animals their energy encapsulates the energy of bears everywhere, they represent an archetype and I use a capital letter to 'name' them Bear, Lion, Eagle etc.)

"It is part of your safety. It protects you and provides for you. It feels ignored and is asking that you commit".

Ben did indeed know Bear. He had known Bear all his life, playing with him (as an imaginary friend) as a child, dreaming of him and picturing him when he needed to rise up and stamp his authority on a situation.

Ben the cynic, was keenly away of this dominant power animal in his energy.

He opened up a little bit and we spent the rest of the session talking about how Bear could assist Ben going forward. Ben left the session knowing he was never alone. Bear was there for him (not just in his imagination) and he could connect with his energy when he needed to balance his boundaries, find strength of mind and protect and provide for his family.

Ben did not visit me again, but he did honour me with an email.

'Dear Sarah, I bet you are surprised to hear from me. I am a bit surprised to be writing to you. I know our session was not easy, I wanted to thank you for recognising me. My Bear has become a dinner party talking piece, as have you. Whenever life gets tricky, and I feel burdened and angry, I find myself asking you to bring Bear. He comes and I feel better. It sounds ridiculous to me on one level, but perfectly right on another. Anyway, you have changed me, subtly but definitely. Regards. Ben.'

Practical applications

- Notice animals you see around you on a daily basis.
- Are there more than three together?
- Sit in meditation with them.
- What message comes to mind when you see them?
- Take action on the information you receive, and you will find your path opens up.

Chapter 4

Earth Angels

"I believe in angels,
Something good in everything I see."

ABBA

Angels are part of our culture, accepted by many people as messengers of truth, hope, compassion and healing. Do you believe in angels?

Divine guidance

I once railed against them. I cannot decide if this was because I grew up in a house where my father, loudly and boldly proclaimed he was atheist, and there was no greater power at work in the world than him. He believed in science and himself, that was all. His favourite joke was, "I am not conceited, I am perfect". I can hear him laughing out loud to himself as he repeated it again and again. Or, if it was because of the stories my mother told me of the nuns who ran the school she endured as a child growing up in Egypt. They told her she was from the devil because she had – by no fault of her own – been born to unmarried parents in the European community living in Cairo, Egypt. Or, if it was something to do with feeling like an alien at Sunday School, when as a 5-year-old, I explained that the Book of Genesis was not real.

They loved angels at Sunday School and the girls particularly enjoyed dressing up in white robes with golden tinsel on their wings and a halo of tinsel on their heads. I was never angel material. I never got picked to be one in the nativity play. I was different even as a little girl. My dark complexion, black hair and olive skin, were definitely different from other girls in my Sunday School, but my difference was deeper than my southern Mediterranean appearance. There was something brooding about me that did not fit with the soft playful happiness of the tinsel angels on the stage.

Angels, in whatever guise they presented, were not my thing.

I saw many people acknowledging double or triple numbers as angelic signs. How many times did 111 or 333 show up for me? Quite a lot. All coincidence I decided, completely denying my belief of no coincidences.

Later in life, I learned that the number 111 or any repeating 1 is basically a wake-up call. An invitation to look up and pay attention. To understand you are spiritually guided and everything is in the right place. Yet, in those early days of my life, I would not. Not with those numbers, anyway. Nor with angels.

The number 333 is another message explaining you are on

the right path. A symbol to reassure that everything is as it should be.

Then, there were the feathers. The cheers and whoops I witnessed when a feather appeared irritated me no end. As if a feather was anything other than something dropped from a bird's wing! The same as soft floating dandelion seeds, born on the air by the breeze or the breath of a child. Nope they did not signify potential, nor were they a sign. They were simply seeds flying to their new home, ready to grow into a new plant.

I did not connect with anything to do with angels at all. Surely you make your own luck? Life dealt your cards and you played poker with them. Nothing out there is going to help you, fix you, clear the way for you. "*You are on your own sunshine,*" said the voice of my inner chatter loudly proclaiming it knew it all. Wow, that voice was annoying.

However, later I read and researched the subject, mainly to prove myself right and to disregard any idea that these things had an energy. Archangels, seraphim, cherubs and the angelic choir were all terms I had heard before, but how did they fit in with me, with my journey of self-discovery?

Well, they did not. I listened to my annoying inner voice and decided they simply did not. I had never seen one, never felt one, or noticed an angelic presence. Angels were legend and myth. A way humanity managed to describe something someone had seen eons ago while hallucinating. Angels did not exist in any form or so I thought then!

Imagine my irritation when I began to dream of them. Archangel Michael to begin with. He is particularly good looking. A huge male energy, with gorgeous golden features and the most handsome chiselled jaw. He emanates powerful certainty, soft determination and universal wisdom. He took to hanging out in my dreams. A presence I was aware of. A dream time experience I could not forget and – although I never admitted it – something I looked forward to revisiting every night.

Imagine my frustration when I began to notice repeating numbers. In particular 1:11 on the digital alarm clock for 11 days in a row on waking from the Archangel Michael dreams. Although, again secretly, I took comfort in the fact the numbers were happening for me!

Smile as I tell you about seeing 555 on the number plate in front of me. Chuckle to yourself as I share the mileometer in my dashboard hitting 55,555 miles; repeating 5s are an indication of change and opportunity.

Laugh out loud as I tell you about the feathers that started to appear in my life. They began on my dog walks. My constant companion – and my doggie angel – on these early morning walks was Coco, named after the Chanel perfume. She was a feisty, West Highland white terrier. Full of spirit, personality and naughtiness. She loved to run off to investigate rabbit holes. Usually or should I say, especially when I had to be somewhere, she disappeared for a couple of hours, only coming back when she thought I had gone. Covered in mud with twigs sticking out of her collar. Silence was often the best way to lure her back from her exciting adventures with rabbits. I had to sit, motionless and quiet, and wait. She was very good at teaching me the art of patience!

Coco and I got up early in the mornings to walk in Church Woods. The woods adjacent to St Agatha's, the tiny quaint church in my village. She was always happy, wagging her tail so hard her little body wagged too. She would run ahead of me, knowing the way around the path, flushing out the wildlife hiding among the undergrowth.

I followed her around, taking my time, noticing the slow changes that nature made day by day. The winter months, so quiet and bare and brisk. The carpet of bluebells that appeared in late April, covering the feet of the trees with a vivid fragrant blue, taking advantage of the sunlight before the trees came into leaf and shaded the woodland floor. The summer breeze gently moving the emerging ferns in July and August giving refuge to the animals living within them. The russet colours of the falling autumn leaves covering the ground until winter again laid everything bare. The woods are a sanctuary for me. They offer a different perspective. Something valuable when in conversation with my inner voice.

I loved this place, 20 minutes to be with myself before the world and my day took hold. It was a place where I communed with Mother Nature, my little dog beside me.

It was in this wood that feathers began to appear. Small, white, fluffy ones. I saw them on the path and on the windscreen of my car. I found them falling down from the sky to land on my lap. Feathers were everywhere but they were not the deciding trigger that opened my awareness to the presence of angelic beings.

On a difficult day in the process of my divorce, I finished a meeting at the Family Court in London. I felt decidedly under the weather, dejected and ready to give up. It seemed the best thing to do was to lay down quietly and let everyone else decide what was best.

Apathy is a pattern for me. Now I understand it is part of the pendulum swing of energy. I try to control, I push, I make things happen. If things are not going my way I fall on my sword and give up. Apathy is disconnection. A silent signal that I am not worthy or good enough. Apathy is my most dangerous state. Apathy was standing right beside me on this day.

All the energy drained out of me. I felt exhausted by the seemingly endless battle between two lawyers, between the Court and the lawyers, and ultimately between us: my husband and I. That day had not gone well.

I did not feel strong enough to field the anger being directed at me. I guess I thought I deserved it. After all, I left, I ended it, I broke everything into pieces.

Growing up, anger was an unacceptable emotion both at home and at school. I watched my mother getting angry with my sister and I'd hide. I watched my father being angry after a few drinks and I'd hide even more. My teachers got angry with the naughty children. I made sure I was good. I never wanted anyone to be angry with me.

I was afraid of anger and have rarely expressed the depth of it within me. Underneath the anger was a deep sadness. On that day, after that meeting, that sadness welled up from within me and tumbled out.

I found myself sitting on a bench in Green Park in the

middle of Mayfair in London. If you know London, you will understand that Green Park is a beautiful green space surrounded by hugely busy roads. It is forty acres of parkland shaded by huge trees planted back in the 1820s – plane trees, lime trees and some of Britain's rarest native timber trees including the beautiful Black Poplar, which can be recognised by its gnarled trunk.

I found myself sitting on a bench in this park, under the canopy of such a tree. Its trunk's quiet power observing me as I cried.

What began as manageable tears turned into floods and floods. I lost my breath and gasped jaggedly for oxygen as my emotions poured out, my face damp from crying. I must have looked a sight but in true British fashion everyone walking past averted their eyes, straightened their shoulders and kept their strides even, carrying on with their journey. Tears in public are not 'stiff upper lip' after all.

No one came to sit on the bench beside me and I remained alone. Only the sightless watching of the tree trunk behind lent me any companionship.

There I was, in the middle of the park on a grey cloudy day in London. The sound of traffic in the background. The toot of a car horn somewhere on the road beyond my sight and far in the distance the noise of a police siren mournfully whaled out.

My sobs had moved down to my belly. They were wrenching at my insides deeply racking my body. I could not stop. So many times as a child I had been told to stop crying, to be a 'big girl' to 'be quiet', to 'not make a fuss'. But here, then, I could not stop.

Then she came. A little lady. I cannot tell you what age or describe her clothes. I can tell you she had soft greying hair, blue eyes and a kind smile. She gave me a piece of rose quartz crystal, took my hand and placed it in my palm.

"You need this more than me," she said. "Keep it with you. Know everything is already alright".

I looked down at the small pink stone. It was smooth to touch, warm in feeling and suddenly I felt peace washing through me.

Everything seemed to stop.
I could breath.
There was stillness everywhere.
I never felt such peace.

I looked up to thank her, but no one was there. The park, in that moment was absolutely empty. No one around me. Not a soul walking from me or to me. The lady I cannot fully describe had vanished. All that was left as proof of her was the rose quartz crystal I held. My mind fog cleared, the sadness left me and as the tears abated, I saw a white fluffy feather land on my lap.

I have that same crystal today. I use it often. It reminds me of the day I first understood that angels were real.

The day I came into contact with an Earth angel, the only other witness was the Black Poplar tree guarding the space behind the bench. I am sure the tree has seen many angels in its lifetime. I am sure the tree was not surprised such grace came to bring me hope.

Nowadays I have a strong connection with the angelic realm and understand these gorgeous energies exist, not only in vibration, but physically in times of need and in various forms. We may not knowingly call for them, but unconsciously when your energy is crying out for help. That is when they step in.

Coco my dog, was an angel for me. She loved me unconditionally and made me laugh. She brought peace when I was unable to find myself and was always there whenever I called her. Well, mostly, unless there was a rabbit, then the rabbit won.

The lady in Green Park was another angel for me. She brought a gift of love within the rose quartz crystal, words of comfort and the energy of grace that washed over me.

There have been many other encounters with angels in my life.

I walked away from car crashes with only minor injuries, the protective wings of angels holding me safe while the vehicle buckled and bowed. I have called on the energy of Archangel Michael to cut the ties of the past for clients and I have invited Archangel Gabriel to firmly guide them forward.

Archangel Metatron is a favourite collaborator of mine. He comes in the energy of magenta pink and green, wielding the Merkabah Cube. A cube made from sacred geometry that rotates around the aura of a person. The centrifugal force pushes negative outdated energies away. I always know when he is around because the colours he rides are vivid for me.

There are other Archangel energies. Each vibration assists with different aspects of your living. Some of them I recognise effortlessly and some feel distant to me. Getting to know them takes practice and commitment, but like the vibrations we recognise in the natural world, of plants, animals, oceans, mountains and weather, the Archangel vibrations are there for all of us to share.

Archangel Michael knows every purpose; Gabriel brings opportunity; Metatron clears unhelpful beliefs and is the universal scribe, recording all thoughts and actions. Uriel comes on a golden light and illuminates the mind with insight. Raziel is especially gorgeous, he is the magician of the Archangels and has a beautiful staff bringing magic to life.

Jophiel is all about beauty, she has a pink aura and brings the scent of roses when she is present. Raphael brings healing energy through on the most distinctive green, the knowing from this vibration is not to heal what is broken, but to uncover what is whole.

Ariel brings courage from within to face challenges and Chamuel reframes any situation with positivity. Raguel brings understanding when there is none, Azrael clears mind chatter and Sandalphon translates messages to Source.

Jeremial interprets messages from the spiritual realms. Haniel opens up spiritual channels and intuitive gifts and Zadkiel brings heartfelt peace.

I joke with my clients sometimes, explaining I will bring out the 'big guns' when they are in the midst of change. The 'big guns' consist of the Archangels, although I do not connect consistently with every vibration. Archangel Michael, Gabriel, Metatron, Uriel and Raziel are favourites of mine.

Using affirmations is a great way to ask for angelic help and these affirmations can be tailored towards solutions. I always like to begin with gratitude when designing an affirmation, finishing with the solution. These do not have to be long, but they do have to be certain and clear.

Affirmations asking for angelic help

Thank you, Metatron, for helping me let go of anything in my energy that is unhelpful so I can achieve my potential and recognise my purpose.

Thank you, Ariel, for helping me find the courage to be myself.

Thank you, Chamuel, for your guidance in seeing things from a positive perspective.

Thank you, Uriel, for lighting my mind with insight.

Thank you, Gabriel, for offering me the opportunities I need to make my desires real.

Thank you, Raphael, for easing the pain in my mind and body.

Thank you, Michael, for walking beside me as I find my purpose.

Thank you, Sandalphon, for taking my intention and connecting it to Source.

Thank you, Azrael, for clearing my mind chatter so I can connect to my intuition.

Thank you, Jophiel, for bringing such beauty to my life.

Thank you, Haniel, for opening up my channel and spiritual gifts for the greatest good.

Thank you, Raziel, for showing me the magic of life in every moment.

Thank you, Raguel, for giving me the words to untangle misunderstanding.

Thank you, Jeremiel, for translating the spiritual symbols I receive.

Thank you, Zadkiel, for helping me find peace in my heart.

Another way to connect with the vibration of the Archangels is through a journey. Use this journey below to connect with Archangel Raphael, the universal healer. The audio link of this journey can be found in the back pages of the book.

Shamanic Journey Three: Connect with the Universal Healer

Take a moment, go within to your centre and your mind's eye.

Settle into your midline.

Call your energy back to you.

Ground your feet into the Earth and reach up through your crown with the intention of connecting to Universal Love.

Allow this energy to flow through you to your heart and expand into every cell in your body.

Let it flow into all the places in your body that you know well and all the places you ignore and everywhere in between.

Feel the space behind your eyes.

Notice your presence, the observer within you, your consciousness.

Look into the darkness behind your eyes.

Coming towards you is a vibrant green light. Misty, sparkling, alive with promise.

As it comes closer, it expands and evolves, changing shape, spiralling around you.

This green energy, the energy of Archangel Raphael is invited in for the greatest good of all.

As this intention is spoken and shared the green energy connects with your body and sinks through your aura and your skin connecting with the bony structure of your skeleton igniting it green.

You are lit up from within.

Slowly, surely the green energy expands from your skeleton, into your ligaments, tendons and muscles.

Spreading into your internal organs filling them with light.

It reaches deeper and merges with your nervous system and your brain, feeling like a soothing balm, calming you, settling you.

It gifts you a word, a picture, a feeling or a

knowing that will help you move forward in your life.

Accept what comes to you implicitly without doubt.

A dark green cloak is wrapped around you, holding this energy within you for 24 hours, allowing it to integrate.

Feel the space behind your eyes.

Notice your presence, the observer within you, your consciousness.

Settle once more into your midline.

Feel your breath in your body.

Feel your body on the chair or the floor.

Connect your feet to the Earth.

Coming back to this place and this time.

Aho!

It is important to note when asking for angelic help that the best way to receive it, is to let go of expectation. Know without doubt, you are supported in ways you can never understand. The Universe and all the energies within it are conspiring to gift your dreams. This is how the Universe expands and explores the possibilities of consciousness, through your desire and your will.

Reflections

The angelic realm is a tool to use. These vibrations are from love, they come with love, they are love. They see your struggles and your trials and although they will never take them away, they will always show you the way through them. Your task is to listen and to follow the path.

The next time you see the numbers 111, or find a feather on your path, or notice a dandelion seed born on the wind, take a moment to give thanks. Your angels are watching, waiting for your request for help and most of all, they are rooting for your success in life.

Gemma's story: show up as your best self to open your future path

Gemma had signed up to work with me for three months. She did not know why she was drawn to me, but she felt a strong urge to contact me and ask for my help. She was a scientist. A research assistant and felt under-appreciated in her current role. The pay was good, but she dreaded getting up in the morning to go to work and knew this way of living was not sustainable. She wanted to find a different way. She was intelligent and articulate. On the face of it, she really had it 'all', but she was not happy. She wanted to find a path that allowed her to be filled with purpose and joy, something she did not have now.

We identified she had always felt under-appreciated. She had stepped into a mothering role as a child, helping her mother with her siblings and this had stayed with her. She did so much at work, more than her job description, none of which was recognised. This left her feeling flat, resentful and unhappy. She went to work in this state, expecting to be over-looked, ignored and feeling like Cinderella. During a shamanic journey we connected with the 'Cinderella' aspect of her shadow, the part of her that believed she had to do everything for everyone. Gemma realised she did it to be recognised and chunked back down, she did it to receive love.

Gemma decided to listen to her inner 'Cinderella', to give herself some love, to recognise all the things she did and instead of feeling resentful, she began to celebrate them. She decided to turn up to work with a beaming smile, an open heart and a happy disposition. She decided she was going to continue to work in her boring job to the best of her ability.

Something magical happened. It surprised me at its suddenness and was testament to the way that Gemma lifted her vibration and reframed her beliefs. One of her bosses noticed her. Invited her to present a workshop to the directors of the company and within three weeks she was promoted.

Something even more magical happened. Gemma was so motivated to continue to live as her 'best self', that she began to practice the shamanic journeys we had experienced together, and I had recorded for her. During this practice she became aware of spiritual energies coming close to her. She did not recognise them, but as she continued to journey and build her relationship with her inner world, she understood these energies were Archangels. Within the three months of our private mentoring she got to know all the Archangels and began to use them to gain information to help others and began working with people looking for divine guidance from the Angelic Realm.

It just shows you what is possible in a short time when you decide to be your 'best self', and when you take action that proves that decision.

Practical applications

- Ask for help in meditation.
- Notice signs around you that demonstrate how your intentions have been heard.
- Let go of any outcome and trust.
- Know you are never alone.
- Show up as your 'best self' every moment.

Chapter 5
See Your Truth

"If you want to see the truth, you must be brave enough to look."

Rune Lazuli

There is a reason for everything.

Catalyst for change

Years ago, I owned a mini. A Mini Cooper to be exact. She, yes, she had an assigned gender, was cream and black. I loved to drive around in her. She was luxurious with a leather interior, automatic gear box, satellite navigation and a Bluetooth gizmo. Meaning I could connect my phone to the car and make calls while I drove around, which felt seriously clever and cutting edge to me! Oh, how fast technology moves on particularly when you grew up using a telephone with a rotary dial and a spiral cord connected to the wall of your kitchen!

I adored my Mini, she represented freedom in so many ways.

She was great for driving about London. She fitted into small parking spaces, nipped around the city streets, was fast on the motorway and had very special – at the time – run flat tyres. Another new fandangled innovation meaning I did not have to carry a spare tyre in the boot. This created space in the very mini car for any shopping I acquired, my little Coco dog, and, most importantly for my bag of Pilates equipment.

Not only was my Mini gender assigned, she had a name too, Bella. I was going through a phase of Italian fascination and enjoyed saying her name with an imagined perfect accent.

"Beeeelllla" and I used to drive around town together. At that time, I was teaching Pilates in South Kensington at a studio run by the infamous Moose, the nickname given to one of the forefathers of Pilates in the United Kingdom. I felt grateful to be allowed to work at his studio. He loved to cluck around his teachers and became a friend. I also managed to land a job at The Harbour Club in Chelsea made famous by Princess Diana years before and found myself visiting private clients all around Mayfair and Kensington offering hands-on healing.

Bella and I had a special relationship. Not only were we partners in crime in my quest to navigate the streets of London, she was also my first. My first significant purchase since I left my marriage. She represented a triumph to me. A 'win'. A message to those people who doubted, me included, that I was creating a life that worked.

She was small, powerful and quirky, a bit like me.

You can imagine my horror when she died.

I remember the day vividly. I had been teaching a Pilates class in a village hall in the home counties south of London. This particular class consisted of 12 lovely women, all golfers, retirees and ladies who lunched. They attended every Wednesday morning at 10am. And, for an hour, they forgot about their lives, focused on themselves and moved through a series of Pilates mat-work exercises designed to move as many joints in their bodies as possible.

Each member of the class had their own inner battle. One lady's son was in Afghanistan and she was terrified he would never come home. Another lady was silently struggling with cancer and the effects of its treatment. (She was winning and won, I am glad to say.) Another member aged 83 – sprightly, fun and oh, so youthful – was adjusting to life as a widow after 60 years of marriage.

We were an eclectic group. Our collective exercise marker, one that the group all wanted to achieve, was the roll-up. This meant lying flat on the floor and slowly, intentionally, rolling up to a seated position, without lifting your legs from the floor. Some weeks they could do it, other weeks not, dependant on the level of gardening or golf.

That day was a lovely spring day. Chilly in the wind, but gloriously sunny, with nodding tulips brightening up the green outside the village hall. I packed up my equipment, climbed into Bella, waved the ladies goodbye for another week and drove off on my way home. I rolled down the windows, turned up the heating to warm my feet and enjoyed the spring air billowing through the window into my hair. The radio was on,

I was singing, I was feeling happy, happy, happy, I realised to myself.

I had begun a relationship, a romantic relationship. I thought of this as I drove. I was excited about it and I felt soft and gooey inside. It was the first time in a number of years that someone had gone out of their way to be kind to me. Kind in a way that seemed to need nothing in return. Oh, I know there are no 'free lunches', but I did not have that feeling about this relationship. This one felt fun, free, and gregarious. Rather like the man.

He was different, a little odd, but I did not mind that, I was odd as well. But all was not as it seemed. I was far too open with my boundaries, far too happy to please him, rather than me and far too easy-going, agreeing to attend events that I knew I would not like. Finding myself abandoned as he socialised with his friends while I clutched my wine glass and searched for small talk in a crowd of people who were, well, not my people. Watching him curiously turn chameleon-like into strange pastiches of himself, adopting slightly different accents depending on the circle of friends he was with.

I was looking for someone to save me, totally unconsciously, but it was there. I wanted someone to take up the slack, to support me, to love me and create safety in my world. I was lonely, wanting to fit in, wanting to be liked and accepted. All the things that I needed to be within me first.

I did not know that then. But my spiritual guides did. They could see me wandering along a narrow path, with a steep cliff edge, oblivious to the danger of spending more years of my life in the wrong relationship. Allowing my relationship with me to go untended. Putting every single person outside of me first.

I did have an annoying feeling of urgency. But why? I did not know. I did often think, *"There's not enough time"*. Time for what? I could not tell you. More mind chatter ran around my head. *"There is not enough time to do what I'm supposed to do"*. And, *"Bloody hell, what on earth was I supposed to do?"*

In true stubborn Sarah fashion, when these thoughts spiralled, I pushed them away, quietened them down and got on with another distraction that occupied my mind and body. This time, my spiritual self stepped in to shift things because the mind chatter was right. There was not enough time to continue to be distracted. I needed to pay attention.

As I drove along the road towards home, through farmer's fields full of lambs and into Westerham village where Sir Winston Churchill once lived, the Universe stepped in to knock me into compliance. I stopped in Westerham to grab a coffee and a chocolate brownie. My once-a-week caffeine and sugar treat. I passed the time of day with the Barista, talking about the weather, which is an ever-constant source of polite small talk for the British. We can experience a huge range of temperatures and weather conditions in one day. My grandmother loved to say, "If you do not like the weather Sarah, wait a minute," chuckling to herself as she did. She was usually right with her soundbites and clichés, especially when talking about the British weather.

With my coffee and brownie consumed, I got back into Bella and drove out of the village, past the collection of tea shops, restaurants, antique houses and clothes boutiques, out past the offices at the far end of the High Street. I smiled to myself and agreed within me that today was the perfect day.

Then something changed. I saw the nose of a blue car, a Volkswagen Golf, to my left. It was poking out of the side road, *"Surely, it was not going to pull out! I was too close. It was my right of way. There was no space."* All these thoughts spun around and tumbled over each other in my mind. I looked ahead. I knew I could not make it past. I thought about breaking hard. *"What about an emergency stop? Could I swerve across the middle line of the road?"* I looked, there was not enough room. I had no choice. I saw my fate.

One last time I thought to myself, *"She is not going to drive out, is she?"*

She did.

She pulled out and pulled out fast, erratically turning to meet me head on.

There was absolutely nowhere for me to go. I took a breath, waiting for the head-on impact. Braced my body against the car seat and clutched my steering wheel with my hands, hearing the sickening crunch of the front of Bella buckling under the impact.

Time stood still. I heard the beat of my heart. Felt the pressure of my blood moving through my veins and from somewhere far away, I noticed a pounding in my brain. I pushed open the driver's door and fell out of Bella into the middle of the road. The ground felt steady. *"It is okay, I am okay."*

Then a 10-tonne truck trundled past me without stopping. I observed it, in slow motion, not registering that I was nearly roadkill. Someone came and helped me stagger to the curb side. By now the traffic was building up behind the tangled mess of Bella and the blue Volkswagen Golf.

People came out of a red brick office building and helped me further away from the road. I do not know how long it took, but an ambulance appeared. There was a child in the other car, strapped into her car seat in the back, she was unhurt.

It is all a bit of a blur. I remember the other driver repeating, "I did not see her", over and over again. I remember the ambulance driver asking me my name and not being able to articulate it.

In the midst of this mayhem I thought about my car. *"Who was going to move Bella and what about my things, who would take them home for me?"* Even then, deep in shock, I was distracting myself from my feelings, from what was happening within me.

The ambulance crew strapped me to a spinal board as a precaution and drove me under a flashing light to the Accident and Emergency Department of the local hospital. No one knew how I managed to walk away from the wreckage, Bella did not make it.

My little car, my quirky companion smashed her nose, lost her face and crumpled her spine. My first declaration of financial independence was gone.

It took 9 months to heal from the soft tissue injuries that I sustained in that accident. My body again taking on trauma and transmuting it with experience. During this time, there was no option but to put myself first.

Bella was not the only death. My romantic relationship fizzled out too. I could no longer be the 'arm candy' at the social event because my body could not stand up for long. I no longer tolerated the inauthentic chameleon who emerged in company, as I was forced to be completely authentic in my physical pain. Most importantly, I could no longer remain in a relationship with a man whose first thought in every trauma was to carry on regardless of what had happened. I could no longer exist in a relationship without empathy.

I looked for a replacement for Bella and ironically, I bought a blue Volkswagen Golf. A sensible car, sturdy and reliable, a safe place with which to travel. I kept it for another four years. I never gave it a name, although it became my workhorse, managing my second dog, Bear; a boisterous golden retriever who loved everyone so much he could not contain himself. He loved the VW and bounded up to the car jumping right into the boot to bath in the sun, cool his body in the rain and try to catch snowflakes with his tongue when they first fell on him. Bear had enough love for everything, including me.

However, I knew I needed to find space to journey along my path within. For my spiritual self, the part of me who knew the way home and who stopped me from getting distracted, from taking the easy route, from being like everyone else. I needed to come home to my heart and own my differences. I was not like everyone else and it was about time I loved me because of it.

I began my spiritual practice. It was not like other spiritual practices I have been taught. This was my way and it served me well.

I have a ritual of physical movement through Pilates and rhythmic movement. Pilates builds a strong centre and explores the boundaries of the body. I needed this movement physically, emotionally and spiritually. Pilates on the large equipment offers a supportive environment with which to reach out, tricking the nervous system so it can let go of its patterned responses to trauma and lay down new neural pathways. These become movement memories and postural habits and allow a letting go of the past through movement.

Pilates saved me in so many ways. Firstly, by rehabilitating my body through five different car crashes (Bella being the fifth) and other injuries. Secondly, by building my confidence in teaching other people how to experience themselves. It can be difficult to let go of what you know. My work with Pilates was the beginning of creating a new way of being. It was the foundation that built my work today. To find a different way, one without pain, one that offers strength and flexibility, you have to trust yourself. You have to become aware of yourself and you have to decide you can change. Pilates for me is meditation in movement and is where I go every day to centre, ground, be physical and whole, even if I feel restricted, limited, tight or sore in my body.

There is also an inner requirement to journey – to experience myself energetically and other worldly. To sit in trance. To be away from this life in the quiet dark corners of my inner knowing. To find and experience more and more of my light.

The draw to meditate can take practice; the spiritual muscle like any other muscle in the body will atrophy without use. You do not need to spend hour after hour in silent contemplation, although if you enjoy that, then do it. Twenty minutes works beautifully for me. I shift into many wonderful places all completely alien to our physical world. They are mini adventures for me, they build my library of experience so I can channel information for my clients with grace, letting go of fear and trusting the map unfolding in front of me in the energy of the matrix.

One of the first times I realised I was 'seeing' or 'knowing' or 'hearing' or 'listening' to energy and effectively translating it was under the watchful teaching eye of Eve.

We were sitting in her healing room, four of us and she led us into trance. Instead of guiding us with her voice as she usually did, she remained silent.

I battled with wanting her to guide me. I wanted her to show me where to go and it took a few minutes for me to sink into the energy and quiet my mind and enter the Alpha state. The state of mind that brings deep relaxation while being awake, and then after a few minutes more, the Theta state. Theta state emits the type of brainwaves that are found in dreaming and in trance. It is the gateway to the subconscious and brings connection to intuition and the spiritual energy of everything.

I know when I am there. Everything slows down. I can feel my body but instead of it being a container it changes into an anchor and holds me to the Earth.

As I waited in my inner silence unaccustomed to finding the way on my own, a scene unfolded in front of my inner eye. I did not see it as we do with our eyesight, but a knowing of what was there became apparent to me.

I found myself running. I was small, a child, dressed in animal skins, with braids in my hair, like pigtails. My feet wore soft shoes and I was playful and excited. Laughter rang out, I realised I was running in a group of people, all making their way down to a lake to welcome a bear. Great Bear, I understood somehow was there. I saw him, as a great brown bear, with kind eyes, a gentle heart and a strong back that I climbed upon. I knew not to mess with this energy, it was very clear there was duality here. As with everything in energy there are two polarities. The energy of Great Bear comes to show you leadership even if that is only in your own life. It asks you to be courageous, strong and authoritative in your being. When you ignore this calling there may be times where you will be sent situations that cause you to go within and hibernate so you can re-evaluate and come away from any steep-edged pathway and settle again into the broad wide road that is meant for you.

At the end of this journey with Eve, I was uncertain and shy to share what I had witnessed with my inner eye. But she insisted I went first. So, I shared my knowing of the journey with my colleagues who all reported experiencing the same vision in their journey. I realised Great Bear had come to invite me to trust myself, my spiritual gifts, and my extremely strong intuition.

This experience deeply moved me. It coincided with the end of my nine month rehabilitation from the injuries I had sustained when Bella died. The car crash that ended the unhealthy relationships holding me back.

I said goodbye to Bella, no longer needing an external expression of my personality, nor a car with an identity. I said goodbye to the romantic relationship that had felt so hopeful in the beginning but was simply replaying old ways of being that energetically mimed, "I am not good enough to be me". But in doing so, I said hello to much more of me.

Reflections

Taking stock in life is a very powerful exercise; looking back to notice how far you have come is a wonderful way to celebrate living. Whatever situation or challenge is playing out, will be in the end, with hindsight, exactly what is needed to take you to your next level of being. If you notice patterns of behaviour, or relationships that repeat like an old record, do not wait for the Universe to step in and crash you awake. Summon your courage, take action and love yourself most and first. Be the leader in your own life.

Howard's story: lose everything to gain everything

Howard wanted more in his life. More money. He wanted his business to grow. He was driven, determined and knew he was going to 'make it happen'. He found me when he wanted to double his business profit in a year. He had tried many different strategies, celebrity business coaches, high ticket masterminds, but he could not break through to the next level of income. He loved his business, it was his main focus. He was his business, without him everything stopped. And, stop it did. Howard became ill. He collapsed with exhaustion. Diagnosed with chronic fatigue, he could not work. He had six months off and in that time his business in the form that he knew it disintegrated. He continued to work with me. It was a courageous decision as income was limited but he knew that he was his biggest asset and investing in himself was his way out of trouble.

With a combination of hands-on shamanic healing and deep introspection while shamanic journeying, we gathered Howard's energy up, coaxed it back to his body and began to build his stamina for life. Howard had been abusing himself, his body, his mind and his spirit. He attached value only to money, only to work, only to being busy, for otherwise what were you? If you did not have money you were nothing, if you did not work what was the point of existing and if you were not busy you were lazy. We found a deep sense of unconscious guilt around success and tracked it back to picking up information from his parents. His unconscious inner talk went around in circles 'who are you to be this rich?' 'No one will like you if you do not pay for everything' and the meanest one 'everyone thinks you are a fraud'.

Howard believed in money as a symbol of worth on one hand, and as something distasteful on the other hand. He had pushed himself into a corner, and that corner had no way out. Except it did, but it meant coming back to himself and discovering the value in his breath, in his grin and in the light in his eyes. It meant re-connecting with his spiritual self and building a bridge between lifestyle and purpose.

Howard did build another business one year after falling sick. This business evolved differently, this business supported Howard, and was built on collaboration, delegation and saying no to contracts that did not feel good. It expanded from Howard's heart, which was now alive and open. In the beginning Howard did not earn the multiple six figures that he was used to, but he did earn enough to support his body in the gym, steady his mind with continued learning and allowed his spiritual self to flow. Howard learned to nourish and nurture himself and over time, a 3-year period, he built a business that was self-supporting.

Practical applications

- When life tells you to stop, stop.
- Continually evaluate your decisions; do they support you?
- Find time to self-care.
- Never give up; your future self is on the other side of every challenge.

Chapter 6

Dead Man's Root

"Happiness, is one meeting away, and it's a meeting with yourself."

Gerard Armond Powell

You cannot escape destiny. Slowly, surely, it will find you.

Find your spiritual truth

Slowly, I opened my eyes realising it was morning. I heard the sound of the jungle all around me. That interminable 'hummmmm' never stopped even when darkness fell. It was the buzz of life, animals, insects, birds, fauna, even the humidity had a tone to it, it was dense yet peaceful. I felt a little disoriented, the way you do after a deep sleep. I had slept soundly for 8 hours without dreaming and without moving. As I awoke a well of disappointment washed over me. This was not supposed to happen.

I lay on my makeshift bed in the Ayahuasca Lodge. Eve sat

in the middle with Juan the Master Shaman of the area. They were tending the last gentle flames of the fire. I watched Juan smoking a huge cigar and blowing circles of smoke out into the atmosphere, one by one, as if testing the air with them. Everyone else had gone. I was the only one left, curled up under a blanket.

Eight hours previously, I had entered the lodge, all dressed in white and supped a cup of Ayahuasca tea. The intention was to see all I needed to, in order to step more strongly onto my path of being me. I had been a little anxious. Ayahuasca was a hallucinogenic, a potent one. I had never been the sort of teenager who had experimented with any sort of drugs. Weed made me nauseas. Alcohol gave me huge hangovers and as I got older my only 'drugs' were pharmacy bought painkillers, which I used to deaden the chronic pain I felt in my body. My anxiety was misplaced though.

The Ayahuasca ceremony led by Juan, overseen by Eve and two other Quechuan helpers was tradition in the Amazon. After setting a fire in the centre of the lodge and asking Father Sky and Mother Earth and all the spirits of the river, the mountains and the jungle to assist us in our quest for truth, we drank the tea and lay down expectantly on specially prepared mattresses, waiting, waiting, waiting.

It usually takes about 45 minutes for the Ayahuasca mixture to take effect. I had been told that the first thing I would see was a kaleidoscope of colours rotating in front of me. I waited for the altered state to begin. Then, I waited a little longer. The next thing I heard was the sound of the jungle around me as I drifted awake from my eight hours of sleep. *"What happened? Why didn't it work? What was wrong with me?"* Everyone else experienced something. *"Okay, mainly physical purges and emotional outbursts, but at least that was something."*

Eve and Juan came to sit with me. We would try again tonight they said, but first Juan had to bring my life force back into my body. Apparently, my spirit was walking behind me, unable to occupy my physical form. It needed coaxing back.

That 'coaxing' consisted of an extremely painful physical manipulation around my throat. A sharp pressing of thumbs into the area above the inside edges of my collar bones. Excruciating pain radiated along to the edges of my shoulders, up into the back of my skull and down the whole of my spine. I spontaneously burst into tears with sobs lasting over an hour. They were not emotional. They were physical and it felt like a huge release, like dam waters breaking free. Juan smiled at me.

"Bueno," he said in Spanish. He waved his arms around my body, clearing my aura of the past and danced in front of me. Somehow showing me that he had been successful in 'jumping' my spiritual self into my heart once more.

That night, the Ayahuasca would work I was sure. That night, deep in the Amazon rainforest, I had a date. A date with my destiny. A date with my true self.

I had travelled nearly 6000 miles to experience this ceremony. It was a first step towards learning the ways of the Indigenous Shamans. That night was the night!

But, why, oh why, do you have to go to Peru to experience Ayahuasca?

The quick answer to that is that you do not. You could, if you wanted, hook up with numerous people offering to host Ayahuasca ceremonies in the United States or Europe.

But I do not think that is the way.

Ayahuasca, or Dead Man's Root as Juan called it, only grows in the Amazon forest. It cannot be found anywhere else on the planet. It is the tea made from a sacred vine, *Banisteriopsis caapi* and the Chacruna shrub, *Psychotria viridis*. To the indigenous cultures of South America, it is a problem-solving tool that helps search for answers. It is used in shamanic ceremony to purge the body and mind of impurities enabling a person to connect to their spiritual truth.

I believe the most effective way to do that is in the Amazon forest. Where the vine grows. With the indigenous shamans who understand its power. Other people disagree with me, but I feel strongly that its energy is best stepped into where it grows.

That is what I did.

I travelled to Peru, not on a holiday, or on a trip but on a spiritual adventure. I did not know what would happen. I did know I would come back being different.

After spending the better part of 24 hours travelling to Peru with a rest stop overnight in Lima, I found myself on an old bucket of a plane. Lurching and rolling into the sky. Looking down onto the snaking path of the Amazon river as it cut through the jungle beneath me. I had my journal with me, a small black book. Not a black book containing the telephone numbers of my friends. A black book containing the secret whispers and longings of my heart. The things I felt I could never say were written in those pages.

On the plane, although excited and nervous, my hidden, unresolved sadness welled up in me. It was so strong that it ended up on the pages of my little black journal as a short poem.

Neverwas

Neverwas is a place in my mind.
A place that time forgot.
There is a tree, a meadow, a solitary swing,
where a child can dream, but an adult cannot.

To dream takes courage, and mine has gone.
Snatched from that tiny child.
All that is left is Neverwas
A place my heart forgot.

Looking back now, reading those words, I am not the same person. That Sarah was a girl searching for someone or something to save her. That Sarah had held onto her sadness for so long that it had become part of her being. It was in every breath and brings me a moment of pause now.

As I wrote those words on the plane to Iquitos, I watched the land beneath me and I felt very small in the world, insignificant, wondering if I had any meaning. Wondering if anything mattered. Wondering if I would manage to find what I was looking for. The searching was becoming ardent within me.

My inner voice repeating the mantra, *"There is not enough time, there is not enough time". "What the fuck did that mean even?*

Not enough time for what, for heaven's sake.

Would someone please tell me, what this is all about?"

I felt I was in a vortex. Going around and around in a whirlpool of change with everything remaining the same all at once. Ayahuasca was going to fix it. I knew it. I had a really uncomfortable feeling however that to fix it, I was going to have to break it, first.

We landed in Iquitos, a fascinating place for me. A metropolis in the jungle, only accessed by river or air. Its roads were made of mud. Everyone travelled around the city on tri-peds. Either alone, or with a multi-coloured cart full of people attached to the back. There are elegant restaurants, mud huts and beautiful mansions all mixed up together. On the river, dug-out canoes, speedboats and cruise ships all mingled with each other. Iquitos is prosperous somehow. Abundant with life definitely.

Bare foot children played football in the narrow side streets. Chubby babies sat contentedly on their verandas. The Western world touched this place, but not fully. An interesting café occupied the main square. The locals say it was built by Eiffel of Eiffel Tower fame. La Casa de Fierro is made of iron and was designed at the end of the nineteenth century during the rubber boom. It was pre-fabricated and carried through the jungle by the local people before being put together here. Its presence added to the romance of this town. I was beguiled.

Hungry to hear more of its history. Impatient to immerse myself in its culture.

We made our way from the airport to the harbour. Our transport was one of the multi-coloured tri-ped driven carts. We travelled through the crowded dusty streets of Iquitos. It was a sight to behold. The colourful clothes of the local people mixing with the red mud of the tracks and the dense foliage of the invading jungle creeping over the edges of the community. I was mesmerised as vista after vista showed itself to me until finally, we were deposited by the river.

Our speedboat was waiting for us, its Captain agitated. We were late. The sun was going down and soon it would be dark. We had more than an hour's trip along the Amazon to our jungle destination. He wanted us to get on board quickly. To don our lifejackets and strap ourselves into our seats securely so he could take advantage of the last rays of light.

Then, we were off. The boat was fast. The river lazily powerful. Reddy brown, full of life and full of flotsam. Huge boughs of trees floating in our path made the speedboat's journey in the fading light a little 'hairy'. I was chilly. It had started to rain. In the distance, I saw black thunder clouds and as darkness set in, our Captain placed a floodlight of sorts on the bow of the boat lighting our way forward.

I do not like boats. They make me sick. There is something about being relatively still while everything around is moving that plays with the proprioceptors in my brain. Look to the horizon was the advice. That will help, I was assured. I fixed my gaze resolutely to where the sky met the Earth only to see a lightning storm coming our way. *"Oh great, not only were we in the hands of a mad Captain travelling at break-neck speed through waters crowded by old tree trunks, and infested with piranha, fresh water dolphin and snakes; we were going to be part of a spectacular display from nature."*

The storm approached and the rain beat down on the roof of the boat. The lightning forked down in front of us. I had never seen a storm like it. It seemed prophetic. The forks of light pointing down to where we would be staying in the jungle. The rain washing away any fear. Forcing surrender to the journey. The journey on the river to our destination and the journey within that I had embarked upon.

We arrived in the dark. Torches lit our way to the main lodge. Jungle liqueur was waiting to calm our nerves. Palm hearts and grilled fish from the river to settle our stomachs. Both were delicious and steadied me. I was shown my bedroom where I hoisted my mosquito net over my bed. There was a small bathroom. The water came from a tank outside, to use it I had to pump it through. My hair had transformed itself into a poodle of curls on the river trip and I could do nothing about it! All I could do was surrender to the humidity, which was 80 percent. I realised that with only 4 hours of power a day, my hair would have to remain in its naturally, authentic curly state; symbolic perhaps, for how I needed to be here. Exhausted, I collapsed into bed.

The food in the lodge was fresh, plain and hearty. Local jungle ingredients and fish. We drank fruit juice, what kind I cannot tell you. It was sweet and refreshing and addictive.

I settled in, smiling at the villagers, playing with their pet monkeys and learning their traditions. I helped Eve with her plans to continue to support their school and spent time in the company of Juan. He did not speak English, only Quechuan and Spanish. He did, however, speak telepathy. Somehow, we understood each other. I already knew him, except I did not. His energy reminded me of someone I admired and revered. He had sparkling eyes, full of compassion that looked deeply at me, not at what I had, but at who I was. It felt uncomfortable. I felt inadequate. I felt I was a disappointment to him. He knew I was disconnected. Even though I had been trying to reconnect to a deeper meaning of me for the past five years, I was not there yet. I was wearing 'clothes' that did not fit me and I knew he could tell.

He gave me herbs to wash in. He chanted around me. We sat in trance together. One night, I had my first conscious encounter of an astral dream. I was aware of Juan sitting crossed legged with me, in the blackness of the astral plane. We did not speak. We sat and contemplated each other. I asked him the next day where he had been in the night. "With you" he replied in his broken English, sending a shiver of confirmation down my spine.

Then it was time.

"Now, I was ready."

Dressed in white for the second time, I approached the Ayahuasca Lodge. It was dome shaped with a fire pit in the middle. Beds arranged around it, each bed making up another spoke on the wheel surrounding the flames in the centre.

Juan was softly drumming. *Bomm bomm bomm*, gently, rhythmically, the sound of the drum took over the energy of the lodge. The fire flickered and the tea was brewed. It was blue and black and thick. It tasted bitter and was hard to swallow. I drank two cups and lay down to wait. I kept my eyes open, determined not to fall into sleep.

It began. The multi-layered colours of light, playing in geometric shapes in front of my eyes.

"Were my eyes open or closed?" I thought. It did not matter. I fell into the experience.

A glowing light tinged in gold swirled ahead of me. Ten energies standing within it, singing the most beautiful sounds. I laughed and smiled and reached out towards them. I wanted more of it, the golden light. As I did my body shook. My kundalini energy roared awake and flew up from my base chakra and out of my crown chakra. I watched as it went higher and higher. I saw it reach further and further away, expanding into everything, even though it remained rooted in me.

"What is that?" I asked, observing everything from a slightly detached place, watching the play unfold without fear, without anticipation.

Patient in the now. *"What is that?"*

"That is you," was my answer. I nodded. Knowing without understanding.

I followed the path the kundalini energy had left. I passed through the colours of red, orange, yellow, green, turquoise, blue and purple. I watched how they merged into one bright light and then, layered again into every colour and then, to the blackness of the cosmos. This blackness felt so safe. It was like the womb space, the beginning, creation, and I curled up within it moving my physical body into the foetal position on the bed. My awareness came back from the Universe and questioned how I was feeling, what I was feeling.

I could not quite handle it. My ego was stepping in needing control. Needing survival.

Fear was catching me.

There was a serpent writhing around in my belly. I saw its shape. It twisted and bent and took me to a place of horror.

"How was it inside me? What did it mean? How could I get it out!"

I smelled the aroma of Juan's cigar. He was billowing smoke over me and the smoke distracted my focus. He started to hum around me. My heartbeat began to slow and the panic building inside me, lessened.

"I was okay. I was not alone with a snake inside my tummy. I was okay. Everything was okay."

The squirming stopped and I was back in the multi-coloured energies of light. A screen appeared within the light playing out scenes that I had lived through. Times in my childhood. I was not reliving them. I was observing them. Not from my human perspective but from a spiritual perspective. One where no one and nothing is to blame. One where there are only lessons and learning. I calmed watching my life dance in front of me. All of the situations I had thought were so unfair; that had hurt my inner child and had left me searching for myself, had a purpose. They had meaning. They made me who I am!

I nodded, knowing without understanding.

I fell back into my body.

This time the physical feeling was different. I felt a bat attach itself to my face, covering my nose with its body, its wings holding onto my ears. I kept trying to pull it off, grasping at my face with my fingers, pulling away only to find nothing in them.

"How could that be?"

I knew there was a bat there. I could see it, feel it, hear its heart beating against me. "Someone, get it off!"

This time it was Eve who appeared to soothe me. I looked up at her, seeing her perhaps for the first time as something more than a person. She was a true guide. She had recognised me all those years ago and she had invited me here to discover myself. I too, was more than a person, more than a human. She brought me along to realise I was energy. A spiritual being living within human form. My sole purpose, to experience life through my own being. That was my deeper meaning. That was what I had been searching for.

The Ayahuasca showed me my presence in everything. It showed me how my body continued to hold trauma and unhelpful energy. I understood that to evolve and expand my knowing of myself, I had to place one foot firmly in the physical world and be in my body. The other foot would then be free to reach towards my potential and the possibilities available to me.

The bat I saw during this part of my Ayahuasca experience finally flew off. Eve stayed by my side smiling. She passed me a bucket as nausea overcame me. I leaned over to be sick, only to feel a huge bubble of energy move up from my stomach. No vomit, only palpable energy. It was extraordinary. I retched into the bucket. Energy moved up and out and I laid back, spent, tiredness washing over me.

It had not finished, my micro-managing character kicked into play. I manically began cleaning the lodge. I gathered the rubbish and debris I saw on the floor. I walked around the fire singing. After some time, I sat back on my bed, my eyes closing. Sleep taking over. My last memory was the green and magenta energy of Archangel Metatron washing over me as I let go of more of my past.

The next day while eating fresh fruit for breakfast I found my 'sight'. I saw the energy around my companions. I saw the energy within their bodies, and I saw the energy flowing through them. I recognised they were containers and had amazing power. I realised how, when fully connected to the planet, their energy was more vibrant and the 'flow' I saw stronger.

I sat down that day in the jungle and channelled a unique Energetic Management System Journey, which I now use to help my clients centre and ground their energy in their body. If you would like to listen to the recording of this journey you will find a link in the back pages of the book.

Shamanic Journey Four: Introduce the Energetic Management System

Sit on the ground crossed legged or on a chair with your back up straight and your feet on the floor.

Turn your palms up and rest them in your lap.

Close your eyes.

In your mind's eye come down within you, into your centre.

Settle into the space within your spine and connect with your breathing. Allowing its rise and fall to become a rhythm within you.

Notice how you feel.

Take your focus to your base chakra, the red energy of your root.

Allow it to open and follow your intention down from your base through your legs out of the chakras in your feet and into Mother Earth.

Feel how she moves up to meet you, gently tugging on you, securing you to the planet.

Lean into gratitude here for all that she is, all that she gives and her unending patience with us.

From this place of anchoring you will see the Earth open up and a pathway appear to take you deep into her centre.

Some way ahead, you see the light of the centre of her energy.

A beautiful white light that glows and calls to you.

You move towards it, stepping into her centre, allowing the white light to sink into your body, your energy and your spirit.

It ignites a feeling of deep connection to the planet, to nature, to every being who lives here.

Stay within this light and allow it to hold you.

When you are ready, move your focus up through the pathway of your chakras.

Past the sacral chakra in your lower back with its orange energy.

Through your solar plexus above your belly button and its vibrant yellow energy.

Into your heart chakra in the middle of your chest with its soft green energy.

To your throat chakra in your neck and its turquoise hue.

Through your third eye in the middle of your forehead above your physical eyes. It is inky blue like the night sky.

Go all the way to the top of your head where your crown chakra sits in is beautiful purple and white energy.

Open your crown chakra with your intention and reach up into the Universe with your mind.

Reach as high as you can for your greatest good and the greatest good of all.

Pull down Universal Love.

It comes in a spiral of purple, green and white.

It connects with your body through your crown.

Moves down through the pathway of your chakras all the way to your base and moves out of your feet into the Earth.

Allow its feeling of love to expand into every cell of your body.

Let it settle and feel how it flows freely through you when you are fully grounded.

Give thanks for all that you have been, all that you are, and all that you will be.

Bring your awareness back to your breath.

Feel its rhythm in your body.

Notice how you feel in this moment.

When you are ready, take a full breath in. Then exhale.

Come back to this place and this time and open your eyes.

Aho.

Reflections

I no longer feel the need to surrender to the Dead Man's Root, but I use its power in my work while journeying with my clients, so they can open up to their higher mind and be fully aware of the magic and love available to them in their life. The energy of the Ayahuasca opens a person up to their spiritual truth and shows them what they need to let go of to step towards their potential. It was a revelation to me and completely transformational. I am grateful for the experience which deeply connected me to the spirit of the vine. I continue to call on it in my work to this day.

The truth the vine gave me was profoundly comforting. Understanding that everything I had lived in my life had a spiritual purpose released me from living as a victim to all that I have been through. I do not know why I experienced all that I have, but I do know that it has added to my personal and spiritual growth and had a ripple effect in our greater consciousness.

Melissa's story: find freedom within

Melissa was a gorgeous woman. Vibrant, open and full of laughter. She loved her life. She was a mother, a wife, a daughter, a friend and an entrepreneur. Despite all this, she felt pressured and flat and as though she was going through the motions of life. She had an internal mantra of 'there's not enough time', she did not know what this meant or what she was supposed to be doing. She did know she wanted help. In her business she was building the financial stability she needed to be free. Free to experience more of life, free to live more fully, free to share more of herself, free to find pleasure and free to love. Freedom was at the top of her pyramid (Maslow's hierarchy of need), but when asked to define freedom she described something she did not have, something that was external. Spiritual freedom, the freedom that brings joy and hope, happiness and grace is a quality that must be nurtured within us.

Melissa broke into spontaneous tears as she realised that she felt captive and trapped. She did not know why or to whom, but when she asked herself if she was free her inner voice gave a resounding 'NO'.

Over the period of several sessions we discovered old forgotten experiences that held an emotional charge leaving Melissa feeling excluded and different. Experiences that she had brushed away as nothing, experiences that were still governing her behaviour. We found the belief that she was responsible for the happiness of everyone in her family and we found the understanding that she must be 'good', that her wild side was unwelcome, unpleasant and should stay hidden.

I was interested in exploring this wild side. As we did this Melissa began dreaming. She dreamt of dark unformed energy, she felt afraid when she was alone in the evening. She saw ugly disfigured people in her dreams that woke her suddenly. Melissa was scared, but her fear did not stop her, she found the tears welling in her often and understood these were expressions of unspoken words and unfelt emotions. She wanted to break through.

During one journey Melissa began to shake, her body began to circle on her chair, and I had to physically ground her with my hands on her shoulders. She was in the company (in her mind's eye) of a huge dark man. This man wanted her to stop, wanted her to stay quiet and wanted her to let go of her search for her wild side. We invited him to explain why and to tell us what he needed. He responded with tears. He was afraid, he wanted Melissa to stay safe. There was no place for adventure, no reason to be wild, these things created ripples and frightened others, he just wanted Melissa to be loved and love was available when she was good. In that sentence he had described everything we needed to know. Melissa needed to love herself and allow herself to be the wild child, the adventurer, she needed to take responsibility for herself in this and break through her conditioning.

We sent the energy of love to this huge dark man standing in Melissa's mind's eye (an aspect of Melissa's shadow), he brightened and got a little smaller and from behind him stepped the vision of a grubby little girl, she had mud on her face, her hair was tangled and her eyes were full of life. She had been waiting to climb trees, to make cakes, to paint pictures, to run and to jump and to dance with life. This was Melissa's sense of freedom. Her shadow, the aspect of her that held all of the energy of her lived experiences was strong, it stood in her way and she had been living with the belief that she had to find freedom somewhere other than in herself.

Melissa went away to journal over a period of a few days, to talk to the wild child that had appeared and find out what she wanted. It turns out she wanted Melissa to fully accept her wild nature and to give herself permission to share her inner thoughts and needs freely.

Melissa's search for freedom outside of herself was over, she understood that quality was within and as she reframed her old beliefs around responsibility for others and being 'too' wild into responsibility for self and loving her wildness, her sense of urgency for life began to ease.

Melissa is still a wife, mother, daughter, friend and entrepreneur, she is now expressing herself freely within all these labels.

Practical applications

- Welcome challenge.
- Recognise repeating patterns of behaviour.
- Step away from situations and take a wider view.
- Reframe the negative.
- Take responsibility.
- Love yourself.

Chapter 7

Being Grown Up

"What did you do as a child that made the hours pass like minutes?

Herein lies the key to your earthly pursuits."

Carl Jung

My main purpose it seemed as a child was to survive long enough to be a grown-up.

Access your creative power

I always wanted to be a grown-up. Ever since I could remember. Although, I cannot remember much of my childhood, I have shared family stories and snapshots of photographs held in my mind. Being grown-up, though was not a memory given to me by my family. It was a recurring feeling, thought, notion and yearning. It was my constant companion.

Grown-up for me as a small person, I had decided would

give me freedom of choice. Something that I yearned for, something that I found was not mine. Its lack built frustration, anger and sadness within me as I struggled to make sense of life.

My name, Sarah means princess. I thought I was the princess child in the family. I was not spoiled, there was no chance of that. My mother had come to the United Kingdom in the 1950s as a refugee from Egypt. Her family, although of Italian descent had Maltese passports. When the Suez Canal crisis hit in 1956 and the British Empire relinquished control over Egypt, my mother's family were stripped of their assets and put on a boat bound for Marseille with £20 and a suitcase of clothes. From there my mother, aged 13, came to England. Adopted by her uncle so she could enter the country, she is multi-lingual, speaking French, Italian, German and English. My mother is not to be taken lightly. Intelligent, beautiful, flawed and assertive she possesses a steely strength that should not be underestimated, ever.

One memory I have, which makes me chuckle now, is being about seven years old. Leaning over the bannister at home, my mother's back towards me and bolding giving her the 'V' sign with my fingers. I did not understand what this meant at the time, but I did understand that I had to look after my sister again and I did not want to. My mother, with eyes in the back of her head, turned around and saw me exactly as I was flourishing my fabulously liberating hand gesture.

I never did that again. Sent to my room in disgrace and disappointment. Sent there to think about what I had done and whether a good girl did that sort of thing.

There was no spoiling me. In my early years, I held a very special place in my parent's eyes. I was the first child. The only child for three years. Then came my sister.

Can you imagine, not only was there another child, but it had the affront to be a sister, another me. I did not like it. I did not like her. She was not the princess I was. Except, everyone – apart from me –loved her. My dad especially. I was jealous, eaten up with it, consumed with it. At the age of three I did not know what this was. I did not have any way to express my unhappy feelings. I had been told to love my sister. To hold my sister. To help my sister and to look after my sister. She needed more care than me. She was special because she was small. All I wanted to do was pinch her and make her cry because that is what I wanted to do when I looked at her. Cry.

Everyone talked about what an adorable baby she was. Everyone smiled and said she was such a happy baby, such a good sleeper.

"What about me?"

Was this the first time I decided I wanted to be grown-up? I cannot say. It was the first time I felt horrible about something but did not tell anyone. Instead, inside parts of me hid, festered, grew.

I remember the day she arrived, everyone around me was excited. To my horror and it was horror, the baby was a girl. How could that be? They promised a boy was coming! How could it be so? I was bewildered, uncertain, how could I be unhappy when everyone else was smiling and laughing. There must be a mistake. We had the wrong baby!

My baby sister did not cry, she was content, she slept. My dad doted on her. They had a special relationship that continued throughout his life. As I watched their bond grow my little girl insides twisted with emotion.

"How could he love her more than me? I was first. What was wrong with me? Why did they get another me?"

All I heard everyone saying was how lovely she was, my sister. How easy she was to look after. How smiley she was. I was filled with emotion and it was not love. I did not know what it was, but it did not feel nice and it was because of my sister. She was getting all the attention. I did not matter anymore, they had her and she was good, better, they loved her. She must be the princess not me.

In my immature childlike mind, I decided I was not good enough to be loved. There was obviously something wrong with me because they had got her. I did not know what that was, but I was not good. That was certain.

Being not good enough for love, being driven to prove I am worthy and am valid has been a thread running through my life's experiences. As with many decisions made as a small child, these immature certainties get layered over time. Other situations that prove the original decision was the correct one turn up and further deepen the belief. Until of course, you recognise, acknowledge and accept your beliefs, thoughts, behaviours and then reframe them into something much more useful.

There were many events which unconsciously embedded this core belief of mine. They make me smile now and I can easily talk about them without any emotional twang or trigger.

The time in school when the 'mean girls' decided to name me 'monkey' and cackle behind me as I walked past them. This emotional bullying turned into physical bullying and climaxed with my head being flushed down the toilet by these mean girls as an 'initiation'. Oh yes, an initiation into not telling anyone what was actually happening. An initiation into keeping more and more secrets. It soon became easier to feign illness. A sore throat meant a trip to the doctor and antibiotics. I did have a tendency for tonsillitis, but this was not it. This was me manipulating the truth for my own ends. This was me getting what I wanted with an untruth.

Before my sister, I was able to see beyond our reality. When I was small, I had a strong connection to the spiritual realms.

Imagine, for a moment, my little girl. About three years old, yellow polka dot dress, wispy curly dark brown hair, green eyes, olive skin. A tiny child, playful, curious and inquisitive. A beautiful little girl, before any disappointment, before any misunderstanding. Before she decided she was not everything. Before she decided she was worthless and not good enough to be loved. Before then she could talk to faeries, the spirits in the trees and flower elementals and the larger angels occupying the garden. She did not know this was unusual. She thought everyone could.

Not only could I communicate with the garden nymphs, with my spirit helpers, my spiritual guardian mother and with my companion animals, but I could fly too. Flying was a favourite pastime. I would close my eyes and go somewhere.

I did not know where, but it was not here. I practiced flying. Flying low along the roads using the central white markings as my guidance system. Flying high above the clouds looking down and seeing towns and rivers and the house where I lived. Flying around the woods following on behind the birds in the trees and the angels in the air before landing back 'here' with a bit of a shudder and a bump. I know these experiences were when I was very young. The memory of them often brings me to tears. A welling of sadness I cannot put words to. The sort of unspoken emotion that lands and settles before you are able to really explain your feelings. I can still feel the joy of flying along the tarmac. My energy a few inches from its surface. No fear. No thought. Only speed and a feeling of being really vital and free.

Early in my childhood all of that stopped. It got covered up with anxiousness and shyness. Buried under clinginess and awkwardness. Childhood was not fun. As I looked out at the world, watchful and waiting, I decided that adulthood, or being a grown-up as I called it, looked like something to aspire to.

I knew I only had to wait. Being grown-up after all was something time did. Every year that passed you got closer to it until one day you woke up aged 18 and hey presto, there you were all grown-up.

There were milestones in my life where I was sure I was there, grown-up.

The first was buying my own home, aged 18. That felt very grown-up. The bank believed in me. They loaned me £40,000 without a deposit to buy a house. I lived there without my parents, without my sister, I felt very grown-up. That £40,000 grew to £60,000 within a year. I sold and bought another property. This one worth £72,000 and the bank happily loaned me the whole amount. My social life grew. Parties at the apartment. Working in London. Driving a car. I definitely thought grown-up had arrived. Then, a financial crisis devalued my home by half. The bank repossessed the property and there I was back living with mum. Not so grown-up after all.

Some years later, my son arrived. I remember the day he was born, all slippery and new. Looking at him, I marvelled at how easy it was to grow a human. I had made another person. I looked at him in wonder. Thinking of the potential within him, as yet quiet and small. I was certain this time, I was a grown-up, for sure. I was a mother, a mother had to be grown-up, but I struggled with early motherhood and the things no one ever tells you it brings. I soon felt like a small child again, trying to colour my first painting and it going miserably wrong. I was determined to be my best me. A grown-up me for him. Exhaustion and overwhelm set in. Old feelings of being trapped, unseen and unsupported surfaced. Showing me yet again, I had not made it to my goal, I was not grown-up.

The breakdown of my marriage was another life lesson. It left me feeling so small and insignificant that I could not imagine classing myself as grown-up ever again. This situation left me desperate to find myself. I wanted to create something for myself and my life. This was a turning point for me. The first real step towards my longed for grown-up status. I did not handle it well, my separation and divorce. In a very childlike manner, I threw all of my toys out of my pram and ran away from everything I knew and everyone who only saw me as a 'minor or junior partner', as my ex-husband called me.

Time stepped in, it moved on regardless. I found myself at my 50th birthday party. Looking at a sea of familiar loved faces all there to toast my special day.

"Did I feel grown-up?"

Suddenly, I realised I did. It was not what little Sarah had expected. It was quite different. In that moment of realisation, I had an epiphany. My little girl all those years ago who yearned to be grown-up, who wanted to be free to choose her life was actually yearning to be herself, Sarah without condition, without having to be a good girl, without having to fit in. She was yearning to be free to be.

There, on the day of my 50th birthday I realised I was free to be. I celebrated that evening knowing I had got there, I had done it, I had achieved my childhood dream.

Grown-up meant spending years diving into my subconscious mind, to mine its coal fields and to find my truth. It meant recognising my conditioned beliefs, thoughts, behaviours and actions. Understanding their birth. Acknowledging their use in my life and then. Then. It meant making decisions based on my now. Then. Even more then. It meant taking action based on those powerful inner choices.

We are all free in this life. Free to make our own choices. Yes, these choices come with outcomes. We as grown-ups have to stand in our strength of purpose and take responsibility for them. Choice is a powerful thing. Especially when it comes from a place of self-love, self-worth and self-support. When there is safety within, the state I longed for as a child can be realised. When you are safe being all that you are, you will be grown-up.

I call this self-mastery. As the years pass, I continue to navigate my unconscious, discovering more and more of myself as I do. Continuing to put to bed past hurts and beliefs that are not mine. Letting go of ways of behaving that are downright unhelpful. Being grown-up, you see, is not a destination, it is a journey of life.

This childhood wish has been the thread of my being in this life. It has pushed its way through into my understanding of myself and my life in a way that can be likened to the transformation of caterpillar to butterfly. The caterpillar has an unconscious potential to fulfil. One day its genetic coding enforces a deep slumber. Inside a beautiful chrysalis, it is dissolved. Everything the caterpillar was is remade. One day, a particular day, it is ready to emerge from its home. The immature butterfly has to fight. It has to push open the swaddling of the pupa. Its desire to escape its past is primal and instinctive. It is this battle that strengthens the beauty's wings. It is the struggle that breaks this glorious creature free, enabling it to fly, and fly it will.

It can be very powerful to connect with the energy of your inner child. Come with me on this journey now. If you would like to listen to the audio of this journey you will find a link in the back of the book.

Shamanic Journey Five: Love Your Inner Child

Take a moment, go within to your centre and your mind's eye.

Settle into your midline.

Call your energy back to you.

Ground your feet into the Earth and reach up through your crown with the intention of connecting to Universal Love.

Allow this energy to flow through you to your heart.

In your mind's eye, come down into your heart.

Allow it to open out around you and bathe in the gorgeous green energy that resides here.

As you look into the green energy you will see coming towards you your own inner child.

Playful.

A little shy.

Wanting your attention.

Wanting to remind you of something.

Notice how she looks.

Notice her age.

Notice her energy.

Invite her to come and sit with you cross-legged in the middle of your heart energy.

Smile at her.

Hug her.

Love her.

She has a small soft toy. She likes it and wants to show it to you.

Acknowledge it and show her that you are listening.

When she is settled and when you feel calm, ask her, "What is it that she needs today?"

Accept her reply without question.

It is something for you to give yourself and in doing so give her.

Then, when you are ready, ask her, "What she has come to tell you?"

What remembering is she here to gift you?

Listen. Watch. Know. Feel.

There is a thread in your life. Something that has been there all along, you may not have been aware of it, or perhaps you are. That thread ties your heart energy to your spiritual energy. It ignites your life force into action.

Are you aligned to that thread?

Is your heart open to your inner child?

Do you feel safe, loved and supported within you?

What can you do right now that will pull on your thread of purpose, open your heart and take you to a place of action that offers deep meaning?

When you are ready, send a huge amount of love to the heart of your inner child.

Watch it curl and unfurl in its energy of soft green. It wraps around her. Holds her safe.

She giggles and jumps and smiles.

See how she opens her eyes with wonder at the places you take her and the amazing ideas you have.

Allow that love energy to expand from your heart into the whole of your body.

Feel your feet on the floor.

Feel your body on your chair.

Connect to your breathing and coming back to your room, to this time and this place.

Aho.

Reflections

Your inner child will stay within your heart. Whenever you feel vulnerable or not good enough, if you find yourself feeling small or unheard, unseen, stretched, uncomfortable, shy, brash, harsh or judgemental, remind her she is safe, supported and loved.

Whenever you feel judged by other people, whenever you get distracted by petty things in life, whenever you find yourself tied up in emotions that will not leave or anger that keeps bubbling up, remind her that she is safe, supported and loved. Remind her that you are the Captain of your ship and you know the way.

Your inner child is the anchor for your creative power and expression. Whenever you want to blame other people, project your feelings onto someone else, or simply feel the judgement monkey throwing rocks from your head, remind her she is safe, supported and loved and all these things are gifts to teach her how to be her best self.

Your inner child is a big part of your shadow. She holds all of your childhood experiences within her and is a wealth of information. Get to know her. You will find the way you talk, walk, dance, run, cook and sleep will all be influenced by how safe, supported and loved she feels in any given moment.

When she does feel safe, loved and supported she will be your biggest cheerleader because she believes everything is possible and she remembers your way. The way of being you before she decided she needed to fit in, before she believed she was not good enough and had no worth.

Allow her back in; let her help you remember yourself. She, after all, used to be able to see faeries.

John's story: overcome the imposter within

John was a struggling businessman. He owned a small enterprise building home extensions. He really wanted to build homes for people that were interested in connecting to nature in their living environment, but he was facing the dissolution of his company. He had not secured a deal for several months. Overheads were rising and he could not find a way through. There was a very real chance that his ten-year-old business would fold.

He defined himself as HSP, a highly sensitive person. He understood that his energy was the driving force of his business, but he could not bring himself around to finding hope and positive ideas to take him forward. Hope and positive thoughts alone were not going to solve his problems he said. I did not agree. When hope is lost, the energetic vibration plummets. I do not mean desperate hope, the sort of hope that someone will ride in on a white horse and save the day. I mean confident hope that emanates from the heart and sends out a message that says, 'I'm ready to receive'.

John was resistant, he was despondent, and he was stuck in a negative pattern of learning things believing that he did not have any of the right skills to make a business work. His antidote to slow sales was to buy a new marketing course. His answer to how he felt was to listen to audios of calming meditations. His go-to method of self-help was to download a new motivational course. None of which he would finish, signing up for the next course and the next one whenever he saw something interesting. This technique was not going to change things. The only person that could do that was John and it had to come from his energy and his intention. He needed to focus. We had to find out why he felt like giving up and why he was addicted to learning.

As we scratched the surface of the deep pool of his subconscious mind, parts of his childhood showed up. Feeling inadequate at school because he was dyslexic and learned differently compared to other children. Feeling anxious as his heightened empathic gifts resonated with the emotions of others distracting him from moment to moment. Feeling all alone at boarding school and covering up the devasting effect of the early death of his mother. Feeling directionless and lost, not knowing what career to follow as a result of being told time and time again that he was not academic. There was a lot of wounding most of it deeply unconscious.

I asked John to tell me his deepest fear. He paused, unwilling to share his thoughts, eventually he uttered 'I feel like a fraud, how can people invest their money with me to build their dreams when I cannot finish anything not even a book?'

This was the energetic hook, the way into his hidden wounding. In a journey we travelled back to his little boy, learning to read, slowly, painfully. The little boy felt despondent, like he wanted to give up. He wanted to go and play, he wanted to draw, and he wanted to build castles in the sandpit. We jumped to boarding school where he had lots of friends and would receive letters from his mother. The letters evoked tears and a feeling of loneliness. Suddenly, in rushed the news of his mother's death. The little boy swallowed and gave a wan smile. He was not going to show his grief. He was going to be a man; he was going to play and draw and build castles and build friendships. No one would ever know how hurt he was, how deeply afraid he was of being alone. He would never admit it to anyone, not even himself. And there he was, the fraud. Living life denying a deep truth of himself. One of grief, loss, anger and sadness.

Once we had uncovered this, and it was a big deal in this lovely man's life, we worked together to allow these locked down emotions out. Emotions are energy in motion and if they do not move, they create habit and addiction to their patterns.

Six weeks into the adventure, John began to receive new client enquiries. In all, four new deals landed in the lap of his business over the summer taking him out of the danger zone and allowing him to continue to run his company.

Practical applications

- Remember what you wanted to be when you were small.
- Uncover difficult childhood experiences.
- Notice the belief they embedded within.
- Reframe that belief based on the adult you.
- What emotion does the belief hold?
- Release that emotion by journaling.

Chapter 8

Follow the Snake

"Shadow work is the path of the heart warrior."

Carl Jung

Sacsayhuaman is where I faced my deepest fear.

Dive into the darkness of you

Sacsayhuaman is the remains of a sacred temple site in Cusco, Peru. It is pronounced 'Saxywarman'. It is where I understood the power of my shadow. Sacsayhuaman showed me how to follow the snake, shed a layer of spiritual skin and emerge stronger, happier and more able to be me.

Cusco was the centre of the Incan civilisation. Today both Cusco and Sacsayhuaman are designated World Heritage Sites to preserve and recognise their history. The Incan's believed that their city nestled in the mountains surrounding the sacred valley was the navel of the world. The city was laid out in the shape of a puma and a powerful and sacred temple placed at its velvet head. In Incan tradition, the puma was a powerful spirit animal depicting the reality of life.

Their culture, traditionally shamanic in nature, lived with the belief that the world was made up of three levels of existence. Each level watched over by a spirit animal. The snake represents the lower world. the puma the middle world, and the condor – or eagle – was a sign of the upper world.

The snake moves with its belly on the earth and will guide you into the lower world. Here you will find information from your past. The puma walks upon the earth and is master of the jungle. It prowls the middle world, which holds information from your now. The eagle flies high above. It is king of the sky and gives a wider spiritual perspective of life.

In shamanic journeying, if the way unfolds upwards, the upper world will be revealed, and spiritual truths will be uncovered. If it leads you down towards the lower world, it will show you shadow aspects from your past. The middle world will gift information for life in the now.

Sacsayhuaman is a vast spiritual site made up of huge granite pieces mitred together without mortar. It is not known how such a feat of engineering was managed. The energy of the place was other worldly even in its ruined state. Or, should I say, ransacked state. The temple was destroyed after the Spanish invasion in 1563, when the temple stones were used to construct government buildings in the city. After the Spanish overthrew the Incan civilisation, they brought Christianity to the people and built churches on the destroyed Incan sacred sites. The Temple of the Sun in the centre of Cusco became the

Church of Santo Domingo. The Spanish not only wanted and stole the resources they found in the area, they also treated the Incans as primitive, pagan, and inferior people. Their leaders and the shamans were persecuted and killed, seen as demonic and dangerous. A belief that has trickled through the ages and continues to be felt today.

Time moves on and brings change. The Christian Church has stopped murdering non-believers in the name of God and the way of the shaman has evolved too. Shamanic philosophy, gaining knowledge through self-exploration to experience a deep connection with the Universe has emerged in our modern day. Many of us in the Western world have found a connection to it and share its teachings. A large part involves shadow dancing, taming the shadow, mastering the shadow or as my shaman in Cusco called it, following the snake.

I was in Sacsayhuaman with Frederick, the shaman who was teaching me to astral travel. This is the process of intentionally, with awareness, travelling into the universal consciousness. He said I had trouble coming back and he often grabbed my shoulders and called my name three times while standing on my feet. I was continuing to have trouble anchoring my life force, my energetic self, in my body – something I was motivated to change if only to save my squashed feet.

Frederick was small and wiry with a contagious laugh and a real enthusiasm for life. He chewed coco leaves continually. I preferred to drink the aromatic coco tea. A brew made from the leaves of the plant said to alleviate altitude sickness. Cusco is 3,399 metres in altitude. The loftiness of its position made itself felt in my body in the form of slight nausea and occasional dizziness. The tea helped manage the symptoms and I felt comforted by the warming ceremony of drinking it.

Frederick was a rebel. He did not like rules. This was a challenge for my 'good girl' holding on fast in my inner world. He had offered to take me on a guided tour of the sacred temple at Sacsayhuaman. He led me through the ancient site to what seemed to be a back alley. There was a clear 'no-entry' sign marking an area of Sacsayhuaman that was off limits to the public.

I weighed up my options. They were limited. Go with Frederick and trust his mischief would show me something important, or stay where I was and look at what was available on the surface. Never daring to look beyond.

It was a pivotal decision. To follow him. To break a rule, to look deeper. It is something I advocate in life now, but back then it took courage. Rules, especially self-imposed ones, are meant to be broken and everything you need for your development is on the other side of fear. Deciding to avoid inevitable change and stay stuck will invite more challenge into your life and will probably mean that becoming your future self is done with a whole lot of kicking and screaming.

Think of the sea on a hot day. Azure blue, sparkling in the sunlight, waves gently lapping the shoreline, rhythmically beckoning you in. You know it will be invigorating, a tonic for the body. You also know diving right in will cause an initial shock, which will give way to a feeling of refreshment and achievement. Why do so many stand at its edge? Dipping their toes in the surf, contemplating how cold it is before walking in gingerly to thigh deep, then waist deep. Shivering and procrastinating. Prolonging the feeling of cold water against the skin before finally giving up, taking a deep breath and plunging into the cool blue waters. Surfacing and agreeing with everyone around that it is not cold after all.

I decided to dive in. To follow the beckoning Frederick, to break the rules, to explore the forbidden lands behind the 'no-entry' sign. He showed me the entrance of a cave. I was not impressed. There was rubbish all around and it smelled of urine. I thought about turning back, but Frederick was insistent. The cave's mouth was narrow. I had to walk in sideways. It was about six feet tall, a gap between the hillside and a granite slab, twice its height. I did not want to go in. Frederick did not have a torch. It was black as night in there and I was terrified of the dark.

Frederick had disappeared inside, and panic was beginning to take hold of me. I took a breath and one last look at the discarded plastic Coca Cola bottle strewn on the ground and followed him. He was waiting for me beyond the entrance and showed me the way onwards wanting me to go first. Dimly, I saw a passage taking us deeper into the earth. I had to feel my way. There was no natural light. The cave narrowed and its roof lowered. I felt trapped and confined. The floor was uneven, every step took me into the unknown. I lost any sense of Frederick. Each step, each breath, each placement of my hands took me deeper and deeper into the cave, and deeper and deeper into a place within me where I had never been before. A sob gasped free, then another, then another, then a scream let rip. There was red all around me, not in the cave, but in the light behind my eyes. I had clenched my eyes shut and was blind to my environment but seeing the most vivid red I have ever seen in my life. Carilion, ruby, scarlet, none the right description of the colour because it was not a colour. It was a vibration, covering me, enveloping me, flooding my body. Grounding me, pulling my life force, my spirit down into my root. Connecting me with the earth with the eternal Mother Gaia and bringing me home to my physical body.

A knowing lodged itself in my consciousness, like a letter posted in a letter box. I am more than this life, I am more than this body, yet without either my contribution to the world would not be felt. I was in the right place, at the right time. Everything as it should be. I was in the darkness of me, yet there was such light. I stopped trying to find my way out. I settled where I was and sat on the ground. I began to see, or I should say 'know', the tangles of energy I was holding onto. Beliefs, behaviours and ways of being keeping me stuck in the past, attracting drama to my life and embedding the idea I would never be good enough to be loved, showed themselves to me.

The energy I received was clearly love in vibration. I felt love all around me as the cloak of red settled gently into an embrace. I felt as safe as I ever have. My breath calmed. My panic left. I saw myself in my mind's eye as a connection between the spiritual realms and our earth. I saw snake guiding me to follow her. I did. She led me down a spiral staircase lit by red flaming lanterns. Down seven levels to a round room, painted in red, decorated with the roots of ancient trees. The room had many doors and in the centre of it was an easel that held a huge leather-bound book. The pages were parchment and the contents displayed via ornate symbols. I turned the pages until I saw a picture of me as a small child with my great-grandmother standing beside me recounting a story of Egypt. I stepped into the pages and the scene changed. I found myself in an Egyptian burial tomb filled with snakes. I was nothing more than 12 years old and I did not make it out alive. The understanding that I was never going to be good enough and living in a physical body was dangerous were hooked into me there.

In this vision, I clearly saw the tangled energy connecting to my root chakra and to my ancestral chain. Not knowing what to do next I looked around. Frederick appeared in my mind's eye experience. He unknotted the energy. Released it back into Source and pulled down more of the red energy. My root chakra filled up. The scene slowly fell away and I found myself back in the cave surrounded by red vibration fully embodied and connected to the spiritual realms and Mother Earth. I stood up and walked purposefully through to the other side, emerging from the cave reborn. A vision of Black Panther was present by my side, Snake at my feet and as I looked up, Eagle was flying high above me.

Replaying the experience, I am again overcome with emotion, relief and gratitude. My physical body became my home that day in the dark cave in Peru and has remained so. Being connected to yourself, to your body, to the earth will allow you to ground all of the ideas you are given. It will open up your intuition and give you a deep sense of purpose in the world. To be connected in this way, your root chakra must be activated. If it is closed or unbalanced it is likely you are disconnected, discombobulated and disheartened. In fact, none of the higher chakras in your body can work effectively without being first rooted with your life force anchored in the now.

Why follow the snake into the lower world?
Why look at the past?
Why master your shadow?

These are all good questions. The past governs your beliefs, your thoughts and your behaviour. A large portion – around 90% – is hidden, forgotten, buried. Every single situation you have experienced is held within your unconscious, within your shadow. However, shadow work can get bad press; it has a reputation of feeling heavy and it can be. If the expectation is of difficult emotions, trauma, drama, wounding, then this expectation will be felt. However, by releasing them, you also let go of the outdated beliefs, emotional wounds, and unhelpful unconscious behaviour, so more of your true self, of your potential and light can shine through your eyes and heart, and into your life. Shadow work is about uncovering the sparkle of you, it is not about diving into darkness continually.

Carl Jung talked about different shadow archetypes, or aspects of self that are not plainly seen that impact how you think and act. He theorised that we as a culture have four common archetypes: the inner child, the victim, the saboteur, and the prostitute or the over-giver. Additionally, we have unique shadow aspects born from our own experience and perception and journeying to help find a beginning in your shadow work can be highly empowering. For what you cannot see you cannot change. If you would like to listen to the audio of this journey you will find a link in the back pages of the book.

Shamanic Journey Six: Begin Your Shadow Work

Take time to settle into your own energy.

Take a moment, go within to your centre and your mind's eye.

Settle into your midline.

Call your energy back to you.

Ground your feet into the Earth and reach up through your crown with the intention of connecting to Universal Love.

Allow this energy to flow through you to your heart.

Feel the space behind your eyes.

In your mind's eye follow the pathway of your spine down to your sacral chakra, the chakra in your lower abdomen.

It is a rich orange. It is the energy centre that governs the way you manage relationships. Relationships with everything external and most importantly, the internal relationship you have with yourself.

Immerse yourself in this rich orange.

Allow the energy here to unfold around you until you find yourself standing in a circular room of orange.

There is a window, a fireplace, a chandelier over a round table and a door with a round amber handle.

You can see a beautiful dragonfly set within the amber handle and your eyes fall upon it.

It comes to life, freeing itself from the amber, stretching its wings and flying towards you.

It circles around your body.

It is deep blue in colour.

You hear its wings buzzing and the sound comforts and grounds you.

It flies out of the opening window.

You climb out after the dragonfly, mesmerised by its beauty and the rhythmic humming of its wings.

The dragonfly leads the way confidently, surely, taking you into the woodland you see ahead of you.

You come to a clearing in the centre of the woodland.

There is a huge granite stone in the middle.

You are drawn to the granite, you touch it,

feeling its smoothness, its coolness, its ancient power.

It moves as you touch it.

A passageway opens.

It leads down.

You look around, momentarily wondering where the dragonfly is and you see her waiting on the granite, waiting for your return to guide you back, when you are ready.

There is no more hesitation.

You follow the passageway down 7 spirals of stairs.

One.

Two.

Three.

Four.

Five.

Six.

Seven.

When you reach the bottom there is a carriage waiting for you.

You climb in and the carriage sets off along a rickety track, it rumbles and rocks as you look around you.

You are in a deep mine, within a huge rock structure.

You can make out pieces of gold and glistening jewels.

The carriage trundles along, until it stops in a cavern.

You clamber out and step forward onto a platform made from the rock.

Waiting for you is the most dominant part of your inner world.

The aspect of you who likes to say no, who tells you to be cautious, who reminds you to stay safe because 'it' might hurt, and who is afraid you are too much.

This shadow aspect is the fear-monger and it is strong, connected to your survival instinct, your fight and flight reflex.

It stands in front of you confident it is in charge.

You smile in acknowledgement and notice its appearance, how it moves, how it talks.

Then, you ask it, "What do you need?"

It is a little taken aback but recovers and after a moment it answers.

Listen, accept whatever comes through to you as answer.

The next question you ask is, "What do you

want?"

Whatever answer you receive, acknowledge it. It will be something you fail to do for yourself and something that a younger version of yourself felt you did not receive enough of.

This aspect, the fear-monger, is here to keep you safe, mostly from your full potential.

It will be the voice which questions your choices or brings hesitation when something comes towards you in life to stretch you and enable you to grow.

Thank it for the help so far.

Thank it for all it has done.

Open your heart and send it love, as much as you can summon.

Flood this aspect of you with the gorgeous green energy of love emanating from your heart.

Watch as the fear fades.

Watch as the dark shadowy aspect morphs into something lighter, more vibrant, full of life.

What do you see emerging?

Who will you be without fear?

Listen to and acknowledge what comes to you.

Thank the fear-monger.

Thank your shadow for this journey and this

insight.

Firmly explain you are the leader of your life and you are happy to have such a loving companion within you.

Explain that in the future you get to choose the way.

The carriage reappears to take you back to the spiral stairs.

When you are ready, you climb in.

Inside the carriage is a beautiful crystal mined from the walls of this place. A crystal that will support your sacral chakra as you move forward in your relationships in your life.

The carriage takes you back to the staircase.

You climb up the 7 spirals of stairs.

Seven.

Six.

Five.

Four.

Three.

Two.

One.

And emerge in the woodland clearing with the dragonfly waiting for you.

You follow it back into your sacral chakra.

The dragonfly will remain forever free because it is the aspect of your subconscious that you became aware of. Free to transform into more of your best self, more of your potential.

Bring your awareness back into your body and into your midline.

Take a breath.

Feel your feet on the floor, wiggle your hands and fingers and come back into this place and this time.

Journal your journey. Write down the answers to the following questions and how you felt, what you saw, and what you now know.

- What was your shadow aspect like?
- What did you recognise?
- What did you learn?
- What other questions do you have to explore?

Aho.

Reflections

When you follow the snake within you, into the hidden aspects of your being, the energy that shifts will have far reaching ripples in your life. Be observant, watch for situations where you can show up as your best self without fear. Be brave and go where other people do not.

Shadow work is the most powerful tool for growth I have experienced, both with myself and with my clients.

Anna's story: meet your shadow

Anna was very successful. A serial entrepreneur with a track record of building businesses to sell. She did that through 'getting her head down' and 'pushing through'. She had hundreds of ideas every day, some she landed others she left. She was busy, hardly seeing her children, working long hours in the day and building 'extra' events into the weekend to cope with the demand on her time. She was addicted to the buzz, to the chase but had no real purpose other than succeeding in business.

Anna was living with her ego (shadow) as her driving force in a constant loop of proving her worth and doing everything well. She did not value herself, her body or any of her 'softer' qualities. There was no compassion or kindness for herself, she was simply driven. Where she was driving to was a mystery.

I suggested Anna journal in a stream of consciousness to see if she could bring to the surface any aspect of her inner world that could shed some light on why she pushed herself so hard. I invited her to get to know the inner martyr.

Here is an extract of her journaling.

Dear Martyr, who are you??

I am the part of you that thinks being the sacrificial lamb will allow you to be loved. You believe if you sacrifice yourself, your true self, then everyone around you will notice and save you. Well, let me tell you little lady, that is NEVER going to happen. The only person around here that is going to save you, is you but I am not seeing that happen, you would much rather kill yourself making money. You make things so hard for yourself in the hope that you will be seen but baby, no one is looking so give it all up. Stop feeling entitled and actually stop what does not work. Start saying yes when you want to without excuse. Celebrate you for a change. Stop beating yourself up about not being loved. Honestly honey it is a broken record that even I am tired of (and I am the MARTYR!). Go and choose to live without me. I will manage, I always do.

Anna could not believe what she was writing. This shadow aspect of herself was running her show and this was the first time she had become aware of it. She was punishing herself over and over again doing everything unconsciously hoping that someone would notice her efforts and reward her. Alongside this, she was neglecting her own self.

She decided to take action. She hired a full team to help her run her businesses, she employed a chef to cook healthy meals, joined a yoga studio and began to practice meditation alongside the work we continued to do. I continued to support Anna for a year, she was still wanting to experience a feeling of purpose in her life. This came when she least expected it and it was not connected to her business but in her love for animals. As she freed up more time and delegated effectively, she was able to invest in a farm where she homed retired horses. She went on to host workshops there for corporate employees wanting to spend time away from their rat race, the horses facilitated a deep sense of calm for her and those who came to visit.

Practical applications

- Know every aspect of growth involves shadow work.
- Embrace your shadow for s/he holds much information.
- Never be afraid, your potential is on the other side of it.
- Understand every trigger is a sign that you are ready to let go of something old and become something new.
- If you find yourself becoming distracted with 'busy-ness', stop and look at what it is within that you are avoiding.

Chapter 9

Whispers in the Wind

"The only reality is internal consciousness.

Your presence is what exists not you."

Deepak Chopra

"Sarah," whispers the wind. *"Sarah, are you listening?"*

Listen to your higher self

Sometimes the wind has words. It is a powerful element of nature. It blows through and clears away the old, the unwanted, the stuck, the dead, and the tangled. I love the feeling of the wind in my hair especially when standing at the edge of the sea. The air laden with salt. The sound of blustering playing alongside the symphony of the ocean waves breaking against the shore. That windswept felt-sense echoed in the shape of the sand dunes, held together with grasses. Occasional clouds of sand breaking free and whipping up in the air.

Hidden in the centre of your brain is the pineal gland.

Physically it is small, about the size of a grain of rice and shaped like a pinecone. It is part of your endocrine system that governs different hormones in your body. It is tucked away, sitting between the left and right hemisphere of the brain. René Descartes, a Frenchman born in the 1500s and widely regarded as one of the founders of modern philosophy called it 'The principle seat of the soul'.

Despite being small, it does have huge significance and wields immense power. This tiny part of your physical body is the doorway to your limitless potential.

The Universe is made up of two main forces, desire and motivation. To manifest anything into our reality there must be both two energies present. Desire is feminine, motivation masculine. Think of a triangle pointing downwards, reminiscent of the shape of a womb; this is sacred geometry for feminine energy. A triangle pointing upwards, a phallic symbol, is sacred geometry for masculine energy. Together they bring birth to our lives.

The divine masculine energy connects to the left side of the brain and brings organisation and focus. In traditional shamanic cultures this energy is called Father Sky. The right side of the brain connects to the divine feminine energy of creation, named fondly by the ancients as Mother Earth. The pineal gland sits in the space between, the connector, the conductor, and the receiver of information.

It is a beacon in your body sending signals to the Universe, waiting for feedback. For me, the pineal gland is something other than a collection of cells in your brain. It is the point of contact to all that you are. So much more than your body, your thoughts, your behaviours and your actions.

I am not talking science here, neither am I sharing studies, statistics or proof. I am offering my truth and my knowing. Simply put, my pineal gland amplifies my intention and receives information from my higher self. That which is all of me.

Your higher self is not an aspect of you, waiting to respond to your command. It is the opposite way around. You are a small part of it. Your higher self is the point of your specific vibration in Source. It remembers all that you are, knows your way and your path. You came here to fulfil your individual specific role in the grand conscious plan. That plan has every shade of light within it. From deepest black, through to blinding light. Each vibration has purpose. You have purpose. You are important. Your life is a masterpiece and a work in progress, simultaneously.

Take a moment and look behind your eyes.

- Who is that?
- Who has that awareness?
- Who is conscious in the darkness of your mind's eye?

That 'who' is the part of you who arrived when you were born, is constant in the ever-changing pattern of living, and it is the part of you who will leave when you are done here.

You, the human you, is an aspect of your higher self. You, the human you, explores and experiences that which cannot be felt, touched, tasted, seen, heard, or even cried or laughed about in the spiritual realms. Being human is an honour, it is the work of expression, experimentation and it is the work of conscious evolution.

Take a journey now to activate your pineal gland and explore all that you are. If you would like to listen to the audio of this journey you will find a link in the back pages of the book.

Shamanic Journey Seven: Explore All That You Are: Pineal Gland Activation

Close your eyes.

Sit up straight with your hands relaxing in your lap.

Palms turned upwards to receive all that you are able to at this time.

Call your energy to you from wherever it is in the Universe, the world, and your life.

As it collects, settle it into your midline.

That deep central part of you that is the crystalline calcium bony structure of your spine and your skull. The electrical impulses of your brain and your central nervous system. The pathway of your chakras from your base, to your sacral chakra, to your solar plexus and to your heart, your throat chakra, your third eye, and your crown.

Get a sense of how you feel right now.

Accept that feeling implicitly without question.

Expand the collected energy of you into every aspect of your body.

All the places you know well.

All the places you ignore and everything in between.

Think, health.

Think, greatest good.

With your intention, reach upwards into the highest places in the Universe and bring down into your energy unconditional love.

This vibration passes through and expands into every chakra from your crown, to your third eye, to your throat, to your heart, to your solar plexus, to your sacral chakra and to your base.

From your base chakra reach down to Mother Earth requesting connection, home, anchoring, and feel her presence holding you.

Settle and breathe.

Allow the breath to fill and empty in your chest.

Follow your mind's eye to your toes.

Bring love and gratitude and wonder to this place within your body.

Lift this intention to your ankles, to your lower legs, your knees and your thighs.

Allow it to expand into your pelvis, abdomen, lower back, chest and upper back.

Bring it higher to your face and head, lighting each place up with love gratitude and wonder.

Coming to settle in the middle of your brain.

In the pinecone-shaped pineal gland.

Become it in your mind's eye, flood it with love and gratitude and open yourself up to more wonder.

With your intention expand your energy from this place within you.

Go further than the edges of your body.

Fill the room you are sitting in with your energy.

Reach beyond your home, your city, your country until you are looking down on the beauty of the Earth.

Send love and gratitude to our planet.

Open your energy wider to wonder.

With your intention reach further.

Past the solar system, the galaxy and into the farthest outskirts of the Universe, known and not yet discovered.

Share unconditional love, gratitude, and wonder.

Notice your expansiveness.

Notice the Universe within your awareness.

Feel how it moves in the infinity loop – a figure of 8 – around you, from within its anchor in you, your pineal gland your universal antennae.

In your mind's eye, you see a nebulous cloud of white and gold and purple.

It comes towards you.

As it gets closer you see it is a temple.

A cloud temple.

It has huge columns of light reaching higher than you can see.

It is built from opal crystal sparkling underfoot.

You enter the temple through the cloud and all you think you know falls away.

You are one with everything there is.

In the centre of the cloud is a glorious figure of light.

Accept whatever you see.

Give love, gratitude and wonder in the moment and come to stand with this energy.

You connect hand to hand, heart to heart and third eye to third eye.

There is recognition.

The voice of your higher self comes through clear and certain.

Notice its tone, its peace, its clarity.

Notice how your body feels as it speaks.

You may ask questions, although your answers may not come through at this time.

Trust you have been heard.

You will be given all you need to know at the right time for your greatest good, your best self and your individual path.

Stay here for as long as you want to.

When you are ready, bring your awareness back to you.

Call your energy again back to its anchor point in your body, to your pineal gland.

It comes quickly from the vastness of the Universe, to the galaxy, the solar system until you see the globe that is planet Earth, spinning on its axis.

From this view point you see the blue, green, brown, and white of the Earth.

You see pockets of greyness and shadow and send love.

Knowing your love will make a difference.

Your energy continues to come back to you through the atmosphere of the Earth.

> To your country, your city, your home.
>
> Into the room you are sitting in, settling into your pineal gland, the seat of your soul in your body.
>
> Notice now how you feel and begin to become aware once more of your physical body.
>
> Bringing your mind's eye into your midline, wiggle your toes and waggle your fingers, feel your feet connected to the ground.
>
> Take 3 deep breathes, in and out.
>
> When you are ready come back into this place and this time, the same, yet different.
>
> Aho.

Do you listen to the whispers of the wind within you?

Can you hear the voice of your higher self?

Do you understand the signals in your body when information is received?

For years I did not.

For years I thought I was the only driving force of my life, or should I say my ego was. For many years I shook my head, emptying my ears and my thoughts from the persistent clear calm voice of my own life force. I preferred the constant chatter of 'could', 'should' and 'must' that I heard in my brain. I stayed busy, so bloody busy and I distracted myself from my inner self.

But, the whispers within kept calling.

"Sarah, Sarah, Sarah Ann."

"Tell them your ideas."

"Explain your truth."

"Be happy with yourself."

"Sarah, are you listening?"

"Sarah, are you there?"

The gentle prodding of my 'presence' became more insistent. I found myself surrounded by birds when out walking. This was my higher self, trying to get my attention. I did not investigate. I absently wondered why the birds were there.

I had vivid dreams. My higher self, showing me the way, offering me guidance and prophecy to assist me in my choices. I pushed them from my waking mind and carried on regardless. Noticing in retrospect the events I knew would occur.

I had coincidental meetings. My higher self, sending me everything I needed to step onto my true path and surrender to my calling. But, like *Sliding Doors*, the movie that runs two storylines parallel to each other, depending on whether or not the main character catches a train, I always managed to miss the opportunities sent to me and found myself miserable and suspicious.

I know I am stubborn and for an intelligent woman I can be hugely dim when it comes to being me. The whispers never stopped, but I only heard them when I was broken down with illness and pain. Exhausted from all the drama surrounding me and full of emotion from not having been heard, again.

Do you recognise a mirroring playing out, here?

I was upset with not feeling heard and, there I was, not listening to the whispers of the wind.

Only when surrender was all that was available to me, did I turn to listen to the peace within me. Eve called it 'my cracking open' and for me it meant my breaking point, any subconscious armouring around me began to thin, weaken, and dissolve, revealing the vulnerabilities beneath it.

Although I had moments of deep connection, I had resisted the pull for many years of my life.

I remember a netball match around the age of 11. I was at Primary School, popular then and head of the yellow team. But on this occasion, I could not get into the game and I kept letting my opposite wing attack get past me. Whatever I did she managed to outwit me. My teammates were disgruntled. Their heads almost dropping, we were losing, and I was not helping.

"Focus," I thought, *"you can change this game around."*

"Jump," the whisper instructed.

I felt goose bumps down my arms and spine. I jumped. High. Higher than I thought I could and I caught the ball. Yes, I caught the ball.

I.
Caught.
The.
Ball.

Inside, I was celebrating, cheerleaders were dancing in my chest. I. Caught. The. Ball.

It changed the play of the game. We did not win, but we did not lose. At the end of the match I was sparkling, that is the only way I can describe it. I felt sparkly.

A few years later, a high jump sports event brought on the same feeling.

"Jump," said the whisper.

My spine tingled and my arms felt lighter as I Fosbury Flopped over the bar and won the competition.

These moments of clarity and potential come to me easily when I am moving my body. I loved to dance as a teenager, ballet, tap and modern jazz. I heard the whisper then and I felt the sparkles within.

Studying for exams also brought me satisfaction. The good girl in me revelling in being good enough to do well. I always trusted myself enough to score highly, even though I had often only read the relevant book the night before. Somehow, photographing exactly the right information into my brain ensuring I always passed.

As I got older though I heard these whispers less. I found movement difficult after different accidents and injuries and although I became disconnected from her, my higher self never left me. I decided unconsciously that life was easier without her. I did not have to jump, win, succeed or shine. I closed the sliding door to my potential and opened the one to mistrust and control. Until it felt like I could not go on.

On that significant day, August 27th , on my 30th birthday, I was staring at myself in the mirror lost and lonely. The mean voice inside my head loudly proclaiming my fate. My heart empty and closed to my life. Questions running around my mind.

I looked up, talking to the ceiling, the heavens, a place far away in the Universe, talking to something I thought was bigger than me.

"Show me the way back to me," I pleaded.

Then, I ran a brush through my hair. Put some lipstick on and went downstairs. My little dog Coco ran up to me wagging her tail. I knew her language. Take me for a walk she was saying. I could never resist her little face. All white with endearing brown eyes and moist nose.

I went to the cupboard picked up her lead, hooked it on her collar and walked out of the house. Across the road was a golf course with a wood. She was happy. I was calm. The trees always pulled down a feeling of tranquillity for me. I talked to them as I walked along the pathway. They knew me by now, probably raising their eyebrows in a tree sort of way as I approached, knowing that I had not been listening. Today was no different, except I had entered a new decade. Time was moving on. When would I look up and look beyond?

I walked deeper into the wood. Coco snuffling into the ferns, her white tail poking out showing me where she was. Occasionally she looked up, checking I was there, racing to catch me, always happy.

I turned a corner and the pathway narrowed until I was walking under an archway created by the boughs of the trees. The day felt very still. It was hot for late Summer. Suddenly in front of me a woman appeared or an apparition of a woman.

Tall, blonde flowing hair, green gown merging with the ferns and trees all around her.

I stopped. She stopped. I smiled. She smiled and then the wind came. Blowing around my ankles. Rising up my legs and around my body, lifting my arms as though I had wings, rising around my head and filling my ears.

"Sarah, are you listening?"

This time I answered,

"Yes. I am listening."

My body was on fire. Not only goose bumps or spine tingles, but this time there was a furnace of heat, rising up from the ground, filling me with intention.

I felt the power of me. Fear came and the vision started to fade. I pushed the fear aside.

"Sarah, are you listening?"

"Yes. I am listening."

As the heat took over my body, everything I knew about myself was burned away, leaving only the ability for truth.

"Sarah, are you listening?"

"Yes. I am listening."

There, in the woods. In the presence of my little white dog, and the vision of my higher self I grounded that earlier decision to find my way back to me and committed to myself. I looked up to the sky, through the branches of the trees, extensions of the flowing hair of the apparition in front of me. I felt myself expanding and for a split second I was everything. The sky. The Earth. The rivers and oceans, animals, trees and plants.

I was filled with light, immense light. I was the light.

This feeling though powerful, was fleeting. And as I came back to my body the apparition faded. She vanished as I shook my head and blinked. My breath was a little raggedy and I sat down feeling dizzy. I blinked again and looked around me. Coco came and licked my nose, sweet of her but not my favourite thing. Somehow it helped to bring me back. The woods were the same, green and luxuriant. The sky had not fallen in. It carried on being the sky, up there, high up. My feet, encased in blue wellingtons, were on the ground.

"Sarah, are you listening?" the wind whispered.

This time I was sure.

"Yes. I am listening."

I've been listening ever since.

Reflections

We are never alone. We are always supported in ways that we cannot understand. We are not only human, we are spiritual and the spiritual part of us is the higher aspect, the part of us that knows all we need to. Our human is a small piece of our whole, walking on the Earth as a means of feeling. Spiritual energy cannot take form in matter, only human consciousness can facilitate that. Our human being is the way that spiritual consciousness grows. Through experiencing emotions in the physical.

The feeling of separation we have from each other is an illusion, the feeling of separation we have from spirit, source, the one, God (whatever you call it), is an illusion. We are vehicles of the Universe, we in our own small individual way contribute to the matrix of energy that makes up everything. Our thoughts matter, our actions matter, our beliefs and behaviours hold weight. It makes sense to me, therefore, to continually strive to improve, to refine and to lift our energetic vibration so that we can unite every aspect of ourselves. Human and spiritual as one and live a life connected and whole. We are on this Earth for but a moment; live your best life with all your being.

Zara's story: meet your higher self

I run retreats in Ibiza annually. I enjoy hosting them immensely and the clients that attend shift through so many layers of excuses and conditioning, they go back changed forever. Zara attended such a retreat. I knew her very well. She had been a client for over a year and her growth was immense. At our first meeting she was a stay at home mother, looking after two small children under the age of 5. She had made a decision to work from home as a consultant and was eager to begin my mentoring programme as she knew from previous experience that having a mentor in the background was a game-changer in terms of growth.

A year in, she decided to make the trip to Ibiza and spend four days immersed in spiritual development work with seven other people. One of the group shamanic journeys took us to meet our spiritual essence. It was a very moving experience and at the end I invited the group to share what had come through for them.

Zara's experience had a profound effect upon her. She easily connected within the journey, following the guidance of my voice that led everyone from their heart chakra through their energy field of love and into a woodland of ancient trees. A pathway led us into a clearing within the woodland; it was dark, but the clearing was lit by a moonbeam shining down and illuminating everything in silvery light. For Zara, standing in the centre of the clearing was a vision of herself. Not Zara as she was now, but Zara in a long gown of green, with long white hair that sparkled in the moonlight. Zara knew this was a vision of her higher self, the spiritual essence of her that knew her way, that was patient and wise and that guided her softly through her life. Sending her exactly the challenges she needed in order to grow into who she was to become. Zara recognised her own soul and cried humble tears of joy in the remembrance of who she really is. She vowed to return to her life with that white-haired vision of herself tattooed on her heart and behind her eyes.

Zara's life has not changed that much. She is still a stay at home mother to two children, she still runs her consulting agency part-time. She is, however, confident in her choices, listens to her inner guidance, connects effortlessly with the energy of her higher self and enjoys living her spiritual life.

Practical applications

- Know you are more than your body.
- Know you are more than your mind.
- Understand we are all connected.
- Choose your thoughts, actions, and behaviours wisely as they have impact.
- Love.
- Love.
- Love.

Chapter 10

Being Brave Enough

"The future belongs to those who believe in the beauty of their dreams." Eleanor Roosevelt

Live your future self

I lay on the bed in my hotel room with the sound of fireworks banging and fizzing outside my window in the mid-summer heat of the festival of Ferragosto. It was August 15th, I was in Ischia, an Italian island off the coast of Naples not far from Capri. Ferragosto is a national holiday in the height of the Italian summer. The locals celebrate this day with family, eating lunch, playing in nature and with fireworks at midnight.

I pinched myself hard on the thigh. Yes, I could feel it, I was awake, this was not a dream, it was real. I was in Italy, on a beautiful volcanic island having spent the day on a yacht with a group of people I hardly knew. The pyrotechnics lit up the sky once more and I was reminded of the images I saw with Ayahuasca, the kaleidoscope of colours, the vivid explosions of cosmic circles and then quiet. I remembered the first time I felt connected to the truth of me, how the plant in the jungle showed me my spiritual self.

Music played in the square beneath my window and I knew my companions were dancing, enjoying the last moments of the evening. I had retired early, full of delicious pasta, red wine and excitement. I was on an adventure, I felt completely out of my depth. I had lived the day authentically me and there was no 'train wreck', the sky did not collapse. I enjoyed every moment. I found my 'genius' and said goodbye to my 'freak'. I had been liked and even more important, I had liked me too. I had spent a day in the company of my true self in all her glory, no hiding, no masking, simply being me. A little cheeky, spontaneous, insightful, funny, warm, open, wise. And, oh boy, did it feel good.

Some months earlier while I was living in Kensington, I had been introduced to Francisco, an Italian man living in London. A banker in the years when the world was struggling to recover from the meltdown caused by the collapse of Barings. He was not happy. In fact, at the time I met him, he was nursing a drink, his eyes downcast and a heaviness on his shoulders. It was his 40th birthday, as well as Christmas Eve. He thought his marriage was over, he did not know what to do. We were chatting over drinks and he asked my advice. To go back to Italy or stay in London. Whatever you decide, I told him, ensure you take responsibility for your choice and live in the best way possible. Do not go back to Italy half-heartedly with resentment, and do not stay in London longing for your marriage. Choose one and then be happy.

Francisco did choose and weeks later, fired up with re-kindled love and passion for his wife, invited me to a party in Ischia with some of his friends. Would I like to go? Absolutely. And, here I was. At a weekend party in Italy. Little old me, Sarah from Croydon, the girl who thought she had to fit in in order to be accepted had managed to find herself here, in Ischia.

The first morning the sunshine beat down on the sea making crystal lights glisten on the rippling waves. A gentle breeze pulled at my hair and I found myself at Ischia Porto sitting on a graffitied bench, waiting. The scratchy black writing scrawled on the bench was in Italian but I made out two lines: '*Mi hai insegnato come amarti ora insegnami come lasciarti*' - an unknown author had left their longing on a bench. Roughly translated it means: 'You taught me how to love you, now teach me how to leave you'. I imagined a young man, in love for the first time, caught up in romance, slighted by his paramour. I could sense his anguish and sadness in the two lines of verse. I wrote them down in the little notepad I travelled with, my own heart touched by them, the words linking me momentarily to past loves lost. I lingered on the words for a few more seconds, feeling their poignancy, understanding that I too had to learn to leave the little old Sarah behind, she had served her purpose. It was time to let her go. That was why I was there, I had taken a risk, coming to a foreign country with people who were strangers to me. I noted that learning within, made a mark on my heart decided to be gentle with myself and then I moved my attention to the wider surroundings of the harbour.

It was busy, fishermen landing their catches on the quayside, octopus, red snapper, sea bass, all lined up on the dock. It was noisy, the chatter of restaurant owners haggling to buy the best fish, gesticulating wildly with their arms, talking quickly and loudly in Italian. There was movement, motorbikes buzzing up and down the harbour and lines of taxis waiting to pick up tourists arriving from the ferries. I wanted to blend in, but I did not. I was wearing belted denim shorts, a blue cotton vest, sparkly flipflops and sunglasses. They all shouted 'tourist'. In my beach bag I had a towel and a bikini, a pen, my notebook and a packet of chewing gum.

I felt decidedly exposed, conspicuous and compromised by my inability to speak anything other than English. How would I manage the day, let alone the weekend? I could feel my mind coming up with excuses to stay at the hotel, including, I had a migraine; my back hurt; I felt sea -sick; my internal struggle was intense. The familiar battle within to stay safe in my habits of the past or to find the courage to try something new carried on. What should I do? Cast myself off with these strangers? What would I talk about? Would they like me? Would I like them?

The anxiety was real. It must have shown in my face because my companions came and sat with me, talking in English, casually chatting about the day ahead. Swimming in Baia di Sorgeto, an intimate cove with a bubbling thermal spring. Sailing around the island for a coastal view of the rocks, and lunch in an isolated restaurant, only accessed via boat. It did sound lovely. I relaxed and decided to go. I chose to be free, to be me and to have fun whatever happened.

We boarded the boat. A yacht by my standards. Easily accommodating six people. I was, it seemed looking back, on a 'blind-date' paired with Antonio, the only man without a wife. He had green eyes that matched the green of the sea. I noticed him. He was in good shape. Fit, toned, well-heeled with a naughtiness in his smile that was contagious. I smiled back.

The boat set off, out of the harbour. We messed about on the sea as only boats can, following the coastline, stopping to snorkel, to sip champagne and talk together about life. Lunchtime came and we moored in a cove with a restaurant perched on the rocks. Restaurant was a loose description; it looked like a wooden shack, with a wobbly, rickety jetty smoke rising from the grill behind the entrance. There was a solitary table set underneath an awning to offer some shade from the midday sun. The menu was simple, one dish, *Frutti di Mare.* White wine and a bowl of peaches were already on the table, together with ice, olives and bread. Its authentic, rustic simplicity was rubbing off. Every layer of little old Sarah was falling to the Earth, no one knew me here, I could reinvent myself, I could show them me.

The Italian way is one of enjoyment, the bread laden with olive oil vanished, the olives disappeared too, as we looked out to sea to the horizon. The wine was poured, peaches added for a little sweetness (ah, that's what they were for!) and ice to give it a chill and as our food arrived it was decided we would each make a toast, 'To the table' was one; 'To the day' another; 'To the Universe' was Antonio's with a wink at me. I, however, do not know what came over me (except I do; it was all that I am, my intuitive self, my higher consciousness), said in Italian as though it was my mother tongue.

'L'amor che move il sole e l'altre stelle.'

There it was again, the quote from Dante's "The Divine Comedy": 'The love that moves the sun and other stars' the final line of "Paradiso", the one that had touched my heart. Everyone at lunch stopped and looked at me. I held my breath, feeling their gaze. Had I been too much for them? Had I gone overboard and spoiled the lightness of the energy? No. My companions, raised their glasses, looked me in the eye and toasted, *'Saluti'*.

I exhaled. I was shaking a little. The energy that is me coursing through my body and making itself felt.

The rest of the day was one I will never forget. I felt in flow, having fun with these people was effortless, everything was about pleasure and comfort. Everything brought me joy. I got a little tipsy, I let my hair take on the windswept boat hair style, I stayed covered in salt from the sea. I indulged myself in three types of Italian cake and coffee and peppermint tea because I could not decide which to choose. I bought a T-shirt and a dress. I walked with Antonio to the top of the island, gently traversing the stone streets, with no expectation of conversation. I bathed in the thermal baths and rushed to change for dinner. Donned a black silk dress that felt quirky yet elegant, watched the sunset and once again had to pinch myself to make sure I was not dreaming.

This was happy.
This was contentment.
This was excitement for the future.
This was grace.

Not because of the people I found myself with, not because of the environment, although they were the icing on the cake. But because I felt free. Free from my self-imposed confines. Free to allow myself to be all that I was, all that I am.

It is the little things that count, and the moment at lunch that day may seem insignificant to an outside observer, but for me it marked another milestone on my path. That day was the day when I allowed myself to be seen and heard. What is more, my acquaintances were the perfect audience for my sudden release of free-flowing nature.

I have never told them how grateful I am for their presence in my life during that weekend. They were my first witnesses. They came into my life for a purpose, to fulfil a soul contract, I am sure. To look into my eyes and see my spirit shining through. They didn't stay, I no longer know them, yet they are forever in my heart and thoughts.

Shamanic Journey Eight: Envision Your Future Self

Close your eyes.

Sit up straight, with your hands relaxing in your lap.

Palms turned upwards to receive all you are able to at this time.

Call your energy to you from wherever it is in the Universe, the world and your life.

As it collects, settle it into your midline. That deep central part of you, the crystalline calcium bony structure of your spine and your skull, the electrical impulses of your brain and your central nervous system.

Follow the pathway of your chakras from your base, to your sacral chakra, to your solar plexus and heart, to your throat chakra, your third eye and your crown.

Get a sense of how you feel right now.

Accept what comes implicitly without question.

With your intention, reach upwards from your crown chakra to the highest places in the Universe and bring down into your energy unconditional love.

This vibration passes through and expands into every chakra from your crown to your base.

From your base chakra reach down to Mother Earth requesting connection, home, anchoring and feel her presence holding you.

Settle and breathe. Allow the breath to fill and empty in your chest.

Feel the space behind your eyes.

In your mind's eye and with your intention come to your third eye, the place in the middle of your forehead, it is indigo blue, like the inky blue of the night's sky. Allow this place to open around you.

You find yourself sitting on the ledge of a round window, looking into the cosmos. There are points of starlight twinkling ahead of you and a shooting star makes its arch in the sky. As you look into the vastness of the Universe the ledge you are sitting on widens and becomes a stage. The round window a theatre. You find yourself standing to the left of the stage, looking onto an audience of souls. You know them all, maybe not in reality, but there is recognition and comfort in their collective energy. You find yourself observing the centre of the stage, where a familiar energy is standing. You realise you are observing your future self. You projected into the future.

You are doing a great job of holding the attention of the audience. You notice your future self has energy flooding from your heart centre, it connects with all of the audience and with you. You feel uplifted, lighter, excited. You see your future self clearly. It is no longer conceptual, she is there, in front of you, on stage, loving unconditionally.

You realise your future self is addressing the audience, explaining your hopes and dreams, slides appear behind her on the stage and a showreel of your life in the future starts to play. You are joyful, making an impact, full of love, living a purposeful life full of meaning.

You step backstage and the scene changes and you find yourself back in the indigo blue of your third eye.

Feel the space behind your eyes.

Settle into your physical body.

Connect with your breathing, notice its rhythm in your body.

Set the intention to allow a feeling of deep connection and grounding to maintain within you. Send this intention down from your crown to your base following your midline.

Go further with this feeling sending it down out of your base and out of your feet into the Earth, rooting the intention and inviting it to stay in your body and carry through into your day.

Your future self is not a destination, she evolves and moves as you do.

Aho!

Reflections

Connecting to the vision of your future self allows the energy of her or him to make its way into your life. Slowly and surely, you will find yourself taking action based on what she or he would do. You will find you choose behaviour that is brave, and you will notice your inner thoughts shift to guide and help you become more.

I love this piece of prose from *Love and Other Difficulties* by Rainer Maria Rilke.

"Be patient toward all that is unsolved in your heart and try to love the questions themselves, like locked rooms and like books that are now written in a very foreign tongue. Do not now seek the answers, which cannot be given you because you would not be able to live them. And the point is, to live everything."

It eloquently explains why we live linear lives, why our future is always a little beyond us. Live everything, love always, aspire to your future self.

Ella's story: dream your future self to life

Ella was already successful. Her business was rocking the world of entrepreneurs and she was making an impact. She had a continual desire to help change the lives of women around the globe, to empower them to become financially independent and run businesses that were purpose-led and she was on a determined path to fulfil this vision. Ella though, was not living the 'dream'. She was not walking her talk. She was an entrepreneur living 24/7 for the sake of her business. The impact she was making was at the cost of her own life.

She was driven to succeed, she was motivated to make it happen, but what about ease, what about joy, what about flow? Ella was pushing her business up a very steep hill, just her, on her own, no one helping. Sometimes her business completely overcame her and she became ill, sometimes her family went into crisis and she had to fire-fight a drama. Sometimes she became so angry with herself that she shouted and cried out that: 'life was not fair' and 'why did it have to be so hard!' And, worse than that, sometimes she shamed herself by saying: 'You are not good enough because you have not achieved your goals'.

She sought me out because she wanted to adopt a different approach, something other than strategy and push. We spent time uncovering her deep beliefs and we discovered that she grew up in a home where her mother was passive, her father was an achiever and the unspoken expectation was that she would win at everything. When she did, there was no praise. Her hard work was given the same attention as eating a meal. It was something you did every day. As she matured, she became successful in her career and continued to work - work - work. Pushing herself even when she was flying was second nature for her. She was addicted to negative internal pressure. Even when she achieved amazing results, she told herself she had to do better, be better. Her way so far had, indeed, created a very profitable business but now what? There were not more hours in the day, the Earth did not have several Ella's. How could she progress, how could she grow, how could she evolve? What was the system, the strategy, the academic learning she had to find that would make things easier?

Ella was stuck in ego, trying to behave in the same way she saw her father behave. We discovered that she did not value the 'soft skills' of compassion, love, nurturing. She was running on adrenaline and cortisol and her body was in a repeating pattern of stress.

Once we had uncovered this strong energy within her shadow, we began to design her future. How did she want to live, what did she want to feel, what did she want to be? Working 24/7 under pressure continually moving on with short-term gain, without a long-term vision or plan was not what she wanted. She wanted life to be simple, easy and fun. She wanted love, freedom and grace. She wanted to feel empowered, and to inspire other people to live the same way. All of her future ideals involved those 'soft skills' she unconsciously abhorred.

It meant shifting this deep-seated belief decided upon in her childhood and modelled by her parents. It was so unconscious it often brought up unexpressed emotion in the form of tears. A sure sign there is more inner work to process and that the inner belief was laid down before the child had the means to communicate and explain their feelings. We had to address the needs of the child within, listening to how she felt when she tried so hard to win, honouring her experience of childhood and discovering what the missing ingredient was. Love, unconditional love. Could Ella unconditionally love herself?

This was a tall order for her. She began to implement self-loving actions into her days and weeks. Her future self wanted ease, simplicity, fun. To live that way, she needed to allow herself to do all the things she thought were a waste of time, frivolous and expensive. She had to learn to be, rather than do; could Ella allow herself to surrender rather than control, be passive rather than aggressive? Slowly, Ella integrated a different way of living and a different way of running her business. Now, she has employed a team who she trusts; she no longer needs to control every aspect of the empire that she figureheads. She runs events, big ones and standing on stage has become her point of sale. No more huge launches taking up time and resources, her business is a standalone success, her clients flock towards her, they aspire to be her. A shining light of self-worth, self-trust, self-believe and self-love.

Ella hasn't finished, she wants to impact the world even more now than ever; her journey to her future self continues.

Practical applications

- Look forward to your future self.
- Decide how you want to live, feel and be.
- Uncover the things that stop you being, feeling and doing what you want now.
- Take actions that align with your vision of your future.
- Find compassion for the younger you.
- Understand you are never finished.
- Welcome growth every day in every way.
- Unconditionally love yourself and the Universe.

Epilogue

"Lasting change and personal growth are found when you commit to all of you; mind, body, and spirit."

Sarah Ann Negus

"What is your highest potential?" I asked without expecting any response.

I stood on the stage. The screen behind me filled with a huge image of me. The caption read, "Sarah Negus, Modern Day Shaman®. Activate Your Highest Potential".

This was the opening line of my speech. I looked out onto a sea of faces, all watching me, more than 100 people in the audience, curious, expectant and interested.

I continued.

"Can you imagine a little girl? She is sitting alone in the garden in a magic world?

Can you remember as a child the sense of wonder you had? The focus you felt when playing or drawing or pretending? Can you remember your imaginary friends? This was you, as a child, experiencing an altered state of consciousness connecting with everything you are.

Perhaps in your adult life you have witnessed a child daydreaming. Completely entranced by the colourful world they are creating as they play.

That state is a lot harder for us, as adults, to access. Often the experiences of our lives have taught us not to go there and we have forgotten how to access our spiritual intelligence and have hidden it within.

Let me ask you something further.

"What would it look like to experience a spiritual life?
To live your highest potential.
To access your spiritual intelligence.
I'll give you a few clues.

You would have deeper meaning in the things you do.
You would possess purpose and confidence and hold full responsibility for yourself.
You would be able to effectively communicate from your truth.
You would know everything is possible.
You would live successfully.
And you would realise your potential in every moment."
The collection of eyes in the audience stared back at me.

I paused.

I felt the energy in my body, the heat rising and the tingle of my spine as I channelled the words from my higher self. If I looked into a mirror, I knew I would see my green eyes lighting up with an energy that is noticeably different to my everyday vibration.

"What if I told you that you already are and you already do?"

The energy in the room changed, dropping down from a slight busyness as the audience moved around, to quiet stillness.

I knew this may have been counter intuitive for many people listening. But I continued, spurred on by the goose bumps taking over my skin.

"Sarah, listen."

I did and continued to speak.

"Let us talk about spirituality in more depth. At one extreme we have a man living in a cave in the Himalayas dressed only in a loin cloth, spending 18 hours a day in meditation. Devoting his life to the search for oneness, a cosmic experience with the divine that merges his energy with the Universe and fills him with bliss.

I do not see many of you willing to go for this option, although I could be wrong? A few twitters, giggles and eye twinkles showed me they were with me.

Then we have the other end of the spectrum. A person living as a victim to life, to society, to everything that has ever happened to them with no idea that they have the power to change anything, especially their thoughts and feelings.

And then, we have you. Somewhere in between, the middle ground. No loin cloths, but an understanding that you hold the power to change.

You have learned many things. You understand to some variable extent, your emotional self. You are purpose led and you want to make a difference and give back. You have a desire to feel good by doing good.

Yet, you are searching. You know something in your life – even if other people see you as successful – is missing.

There is an itch you cannot quite scratch that can be felt in the background of your everyday life. It drives you to strive for more.

I know. I used to feel overwhelmed without knowing why. I had the recurring thought I was running out of time. Time to do what? I was not sure. I distracted myself with pain, illness, material things and busied myself with mindless over-giving. All the time, I ignored my real purpose, disconnected from my higher self. When I was asked what I really wanted I did not know. I simply wanted more.

Which brings me to another asked and often unanswered question.

What is more?

More stuff, bigger car, bigger house. Maybe a boat, more money, more external success?

Maybe?

But when you have those things the itch remains. In the middle of your mind, in your body and floating in your energy.

Maybe the itch is the motivating force that brought you here.

You want to know more.

You are curious.

You are open.

You want to find a sense of contentment, of inspiration, of deeply held knowing throughout your whole being of success and of impact.

Wouldn't that feel like bliss to wake up and feel like that every day?

Getting up each day building your legacy, designing your life towards change for the better in our crazy world?

Now that excites me. And it is exactly what I help create and guide people towards.

I am the Modern Day Shaman®. I am here to shift your consciousness. To show you everything you need is within. To encourage you to live, think and behave from a place of spiritual intelligence, from your higher mind and from your heart, so you know success in your being.

The way to spiritual intelligence does not have to be hard. You have not got to have numerous car crashes like me.

You do not have to experience disease, depression or chronic fatigue to notice that perhaps you are on the wrong track, in the wrong job, or simply ignoring your soul purpose.

And, you do not have to trek out to Peru to experience Ayahuasca and learn from the indigenous shamans to understand how connected and powerful you are. I did all that for you.

So, if you are in denial – it's a place in Egypt – the Nile. Yeah, joke telling is not my superpower, but facilitating personal growth through spiritual work is! My work marries ancient philosophical teachings and modern mindset work to show you how you can become the fullest expression of you and achieve all you want to in the modern way of being.

Shamanism is that philosophy. Science can track its origins back 30,000 years both ethnologically and archeologically. It has been around for a while. Its common theme is being connected to the Earth, or Mother Earth as it was named by our ancestors, everything on it and to the wider consciousness of the Universe, which the ancient people called Father Sky.

Today, I use shamanism as a way to help you gain knowledge of yourself by experiencing all that you are in an altered state. Ayahuasca shows your spiritual truth and will purge you of the things you no longer need. Shamanic journeying does the same.

I will leave you now with a gift.

The gift of your breath.

I find breath fascinating. When we inhale, we create a new shape with ourselves. Try it.

Inhale.

When we exhale, we let go of that potential easily, effortlessly, without thinking of it and especially without regret.

Exhale.

We do not hold on to it and think, I want to keep that

breath, I cannot let that breath go because I will never find another one like it.

We do not think consciously, I will breathe in and be a whole new me, a more fulfilled me, a more open me, a more fabulous me. Although that is what is happening. Each moment you let go of the past, the old, the no longer needed. Each moment you welcome in the new.

Every moment you change.

This change is inevitable, and it is happening within you.

I think that is pretty amazing.

You are amazing.
A miracle.
You are your highest potential in being you.

Out of the whole expansion of the Universe, you, imperfectly perfect in your uniqueness have landed here on this beautiful planet.

Planet Earth in this particular solar system. Exactly the right distance from the sun to sustain life.

You are a miracle.

As I finished speaking, I felt my energy filling the room. Had I touched their hearts? I did not know but I had opened mine. I had shared my truth. Not the truth, but the truth coming from my unique life. The truth of knowing my highest potential is now.

It took a while, but I found my way back to me.

If you find resonance with my story and feel shamanic energy flowing in your life.

Know this.

You are not a shaman.

You are shaman.

References

1. "Human beings are not born once and for all on the day their mothers give birth to them, but … life obliges them over and over again to give birth to themselves." Gabriel García Márquez

   Gabriel García Márquez was a Colombian 20th century novelist who lived from 1927 to 2014. He was awarded the Nobel Prize for Literature in 1982 mostly for his masterpiece *One Hundred Years of Solitude.* The quotation I have used in chapter one explains my understanding of the evolution of our lives. We change constantly and create a new self over and over again as we grow older.

2. "We live in a rainbow of chaos." Paul Cézanne

   Paul Cézanne was a French post-impressionist artist. He lived from 1839 to 1906. He used repetitive brush strokes in his paintings after studying his subjects deeply. He built complex fields of colour and is said to have formed a bridge between the impressionists of the 19th century and the art emerging in the 20th century. Both Matisse and Picasso called him 'the father of us all'. When I look into energy, I see layers of colours all interacting in a complicated dance. Shapes are created that translate to life. I love that Cézanne was a bridge. A shaman of art perhaps?

3. "If you talk to the animals, they will talk with you and you will know each other." Chief Dan George

   Chief Dan George was many things in his life, which spanned from 1899 to 1981. He was the Chief of the Tsleil-Waututh First Nation whose Indian reserve is in North Vancouver, British Colombia. He was also an actor, musician, poet and author. However, he is best known for his movie roles. He starred opposite Dustin Hoffman in *Little Big Man* in 1970, for which he was nominated for an Academy Award for best supporting actor and alongside Clint Eastwood in *The Outlaw Josey Wales* in 1976. He used his fame to educate Westerners about the plight of the Native Americans. His books were posthumously combined and published by Hancock House, to form *The Best of Chief Dan George*, which became a bestseller.

   The Native American people hold a special reverence for the animals of their world. The totem pole was carved to honour the animals holding the energy of their tribe, a totem animal depicts a tribe, whereas a power animal brings specific information for individuals.

4. "I believe in angels. Something good in everything I see." ABBA

   ABBA are a Swedish Pop group formed in 1972. Their songs were written and sung in English, their second language. They became one of the most successful acts in the history of pop culture. I grew up listening to their music. Their song, *I Believe In Angels* has always been a favourite of mine. I play it when I need to remind myself that I am not the only one who believes there is more than we see in our reality.

5. "If you want the truth you have to be brave enough to look." Rune Lazuli

   Rune Lazuli has 71,000 followers on Instagram. She is from Lebanon and I came across her writing by accident, or was it? Her style is honest and real. I resonate deeply with it.

6. "Happiness is one meeting away, and it's a meeting with yourself." Gerard Armond Powell

   Gerard Armond Powell is an American entrepreneur and founder of the Rythmia Life Advancement Centre in Costa Rica. He overcame depression after an experience with plant medicine, which lead him to set up the medically licenced luxury retreat. It is focused on spiritual awakening through plant medicine journeys. I felt this quotation matched very well to my story of Ayahuasca.

7. "What did you do as a child that made the hours pass like minutes? Herein lies the key to your earthly pursuit." Carl Jung

   Carl Jung was a Swiss psychiatrist. He lived from 1875 to 1961. He was a student of Freud and expanded the idea of psychoanalysis and founded analytical psychology. I find Jung's work fascinating and use his premise of archetypes in my work.

8. "Shadow work is the path of the heart warrior." Carl Jung

   In Jungian psychology, 'Shadow is the unconscious aspect of the personality not yet identified'. The shadow plays a central role in my work. Becoming conscious is our overall reason for being. Delving into what is hidden and unknown allows conscious expansion and evolution.

9. "The only reality is internal consciousness. Your presence is what exists not you." Deepak Chopra

   Deepak Chopra is an American author and public speaker. He was born in India where he trained in medicine before settling in the United States. Today, he is an advocate for alternative medicine and is one of the best-known figures in this field. I love this quote and agree wholeheartedly. This 'knowing' has been a lifelong exploration of my reality.

10. "The future belongs to those who believe in the beauty of their dreams." Eleanor Roosevelt.

    Eleanor Roosevelt was the longest serving First Lady of the United States. She was a controversial figure who sometimes disagreed with her husband's, President Roosevelt's policies. She was a human rights activist and reshaped the role of the First Lady in American politics. Her quote above is my truth.

11. "Be patient toward all that is unsolved in your heart and try to love the questions themselves, like locked rooms and like books that are now written in a very foreign tongue. Do not now seek the answers, which cannot be given you because you would not be able to live them. And the point is, to live everything." Rainer Maria Rilke

    This resonates strongly, it is our reason for being alive. To live everything.

    Rainer Maria Rilke was a bohemian poet from Austria. I find his writing so mystical it connects me to the truth of life.

Bibliography

Anatomy of the Spirit, Carolyn Myss

Animal Spirit Guides, Steven D Farmer PhD

Man's Search for Meaning, Viktor Frankl

The Archetypes and the Collective Unconscious, Carl Jung

The Divine Comedy, Dante Alighieri

Sliding Doors, fantasy/comedy film 1998, Screenplay/ Director, Peter Howitt

Love and other Difficulties, Rainer Maria Rilke

Next Steps

I am delighted to gift to you this link

https://sarahnegus.com/modern-day-shaman-book/meditations/

which gives you access to audio versions of all the shamanic journeys and meditations from the book within my website for free. Please use these unique resources to further your journey, and if I can help you in anyway, please contact me.

My website contains free resources for you, designed to take you beyond what you already know and into the possibility and potential of you.

www.sarahnegus.com

Contact the Author

If you like what you have read in this book, please discover more content, resources, support and guidance by connecting with me and other people on their spiritual journey, by using the following platforms.

Facebook online community

https://www.facebook.com/sarahannnegus/

YouTube Channel

https://bit.ly/snegus

LinkedIn

http://www.linkedin.com/in/sarahannnegus

Pinterest

https://www.pinterest.co.uk/sarahnegus/pins/

Instagram

https://www.instagram.com/sarahannnegus/

@ModernDayShaman®

All links to these resources can also be found on my website

www.sarahnegus.com

Printed in Great Britain
by Amazon